On Understanding Understanding

"Thoroughly understand what it is to understand, and not only will you understand the broad lines of all there is to understand but also you will possess a fixed base, an invariant pattern, opening upon all further developments of understanding."

Bernard J. F. Lonergan, S.J.

On Understanding Understanding

A Philosophy of Knowledge

by

VINCENT G. POTTER

Fordham University Press
New York

© Copyright 1994 FORDHAM UNIVERSITY PRESS
All rights reserved.
LC 93-7931
ISBN 0-8232-1486-9
Fourth Printing 2004

Library of Congress Cataloging-in-Publication Data

Potter, Vincent G.
    On understanding understanding / by Vincent G. Potter. — 2nd ed.
      p. cm.
    Rev. ed. of: Philosophy of knowledge.
    Includes bibliographical references and index.
    ISBN 0-8232-1486-9.
    1. Knowledge, Theory of. I. Potter, Vincent G. Philosophy of knowledge. II. Title.
BD161.P729   1994   93-7931
121—dc20   CIP

Printed in the United States of America

To
my students
without whom this book
would never have been written
and
especially to
Hani, Inga, and John

Contents

Introduction: Fundamental Notions	1
1. Skepticism	15
2. Structure of Knowing	35
3. The Role of Sensation	44
4. Other Positions on Sensation	59
5. The Role of Conceptualization	76
6. Judgment	90
7. Complementing the Classical View: Abstraction and the *A Priori*	101
8. Complementing the Classical View: Truth, Error, and Conceptual Frameworks	116
9. Memory and Testimony	130
10. Inference: A Source of Knowledge	141
Epilogue: Integrative Wisdom	156
Appendix I: The Fourth Condition	159
Appendix II: Heelan's Q-Lattice	162
Appendix III: Being Mistaken and Being in Error	165
Appendix IV: Derrida and Deconstructionism: A Summary for the Simple	166
Bibliography	170
Indices	177

On Understanding Understanding

INTRODUCTION

Fundamental Notions

THE "PHILOSOPHY OF KNOWLEDGE" is that branch of philosophy which tries to determine in a general way what the nature and scope of man's capacity to know are. Precisely what this determination will turn out to be cannot be foreseen at the beginning of our investigation since the very reason for undertaking such a project is to find that out in a methodical and systematic way. Nonetheless, even at this point, we do have a vague sense of what we are after, and, presumably, we have had enough experience of our ignorance and capacity for error to motivate us to take up this arduous task.

Our common-sense notion of nature tells us that an investigation into the "nature" of anything means at least that we are asking "what sort of thing is it?" To be sure, this question is none too precise, but it will do for a beginning. Again, our common-sense notion of "scope" tells us that an inquiry into the "scope" of anything means at least that we are asking "how far does it extend?" Again, this imprecise query will do for the moment.

Notice that we are not asking whether we know anything at all. The reason is, as we shall see in detail later, that this question cannot be asked at all, because to have asked it is to have answered it affirmatively. The real issue in any philosophical discussion of human knowing is to determine what is meant by "knowing" and what general conditions must be fulfilled before one can legitimately make a claim "to know." Plato tried to answer these questions in the *Theaetetus* where he took up the distinction made in the *Republic* between knowledge (*epistēmē*) and true belief (*doxa*).[1] The term "epistemology" means (the "logos" or theory of "*epistēmē*" or knowing).

English uses the term "to know" in a variety of related, but different, senses. Thus, we speak of "knowing" a person or a place or a thing, in the sense of "being acquainted with it" or, perhaps, "being familiar with it." Again, we speak of "knowing" something, in the sense of being aware of it or of having heard of it. Further, we say that we "know how" to do this or that, or that we "know" a certain poem of Shakespeare's. All these uses have the sense of having acquired a skill or habit of some sort. Moreover, we speak of "knowing that," where the "that" introduces a proposition describing or explaining some aspect of the world and claiming it to be so. In a word, "knowing that" is propositional knowledge which when asserted claims to state a truth about the world. To be sure, we can make truth-claims about knowing something by acquaintance, or about knowing how to do something, and these claims are shown to be true or false by exhibiting appropriate evidence, in the one case by recognition, in the other by execution. In this sense of the word a claim is either true or false. Our study is concerned with this last sense of the term only.

Truth-claims are always made in propositions. We might define a proposition as that of which it makes sense to ask "true or false?"[2] Propositions are expressed linguistically in sentences. But not all sentences express propositions. "Ouch!" is a perfectly good English sentence, but it does not express a proposition since it makes no sense to ask whether it is true or false. Again, "What time is it?" is grammatically correct and semantically meaningful in English, but this sentence does not express a proposition since one cannot ask whether or not what the sentence expresses is true.

Since our study of knowing is carried on in English, we will be dealing with English sentences that express propositions. By a proposition we will mean what is either true or false. Notice that in any given case we may not be able to decide whether a proposition is true or false (because we do not have enough evidence to decide), but in every case, if the proposition really has a meaning, it is one or the other. If it is neither true nor false, we would be forced to say that some "meaningful" propositions generate paradoxes like the following:

This sentence is false.

If the preceding sentence expresses a proposition, that proposition can be neither true nor false, because if it is true, then it is false, and if it is false, then it is true. We can avoid such an embarrassing conclusion simply by considering any such alleged proposition as a pseudo-proposition, that is, without meaning (having neither sense nor reference). In general, any proposition which tries to refer to itself is nonsense.[3]

In summary, then, propositions are expressed in syntactically correct and semantically meaningful sentences of some language or other (in our case, English). Propositions are either true or false (even if we do not or cannot decide in a particular case). Any sentence which pretends to state a proposition which is neither true nor false is without meaning.

Finally, insofar as propositions have meaning, they can be thought about, doubted, entertained as hypotheses, and believed, as well as known. Insofar as propositions are either true or false, they can be asserted or denied, and such assertion or denial is justified (warranted) or not depending upon the evidence. This act of assertion or denial is called judgment, and it is only at this level of intellectual activity that the questions of truth and certitude arise. And so it is only at this level that the question of knowledge ("knowing that") is posed.

How, then, precisely will we be using the term "knowledge" here? For now we will understand by knowledge *justified true belief*. This is Plato's definition in the *Theaetetus*. Knowledge always involves belief, in the sense of firm conviction. It would be odd to say that I know some proposition, that-p, to be the case but I am not sure. Further, knowledge supposes that what is believed is in fact true. Again, it would be strange, not to say self-contradictory, to claim that that-p is the case but at the same time to say that that-p is false. Finally, because one might, by mere chance or by a lucky guess, hold to be true a belief that in fact is true, to claim knowledge in the matter one might reasonably expect to be provided with sufficient evidence for the belief. In just this way Plato distinguishes true opinion (*doxa*) from knowledge (*epistēmē*).

Recently, this classical characterization of knowledge as justified true belief has been challenged in four ways. (1) Some have denied that knowledge can be understood in terms of belief since, according to them, I believe something precisely when I do *not* know it. (2) Others, following Edmund Gettier, have claimed that justified true belief is *necessary* to characterize knowledge but *not sufficient*; some other condition must be added. (3) Still others hold that "justified belief" is sufficient to define "knowing" and, hence, adding "true" is at best unnecessary and at worst misleading. (4) Yet others argue that knowledge is nothing but true belief and, thus, no "justification" in the strict sense is necessary.[4]

The first objection is not so serious since it is a matter of what one understands by "belief." The second is more serious and requires some answer. Gettier's point is that although the classical account gives conditions *necessary* for knowledge, those conditions are not conjointly *sufficient*. He tries to make his point by offering the following "paradox": A person inquires of an office receptionist the time. The receptionist consults the office clock, which has been accurate for years and years, and gives the time so indicated. The fact of the matter is that the time read off is correct, but, unknown to the receptionist, the clock had stopped exactly twelve hours before. Does it make sense to say that the receptionist *knew* the correct time? From one point of view (the classical definition) it seems that one must say "yes" because (1) the receptionist believed that the indicated time was correct; (2) in fact, the time was correct; and (3) there was a justification for the belief, namely, the reliability of the clock over so long a time. Still, from another point of view, it seems very odd because, as a matter of fact, the accuracy of the receptionist's report of the time was a sheer coincidence. The supposed justification was based on what was assumed to be fact but was not. The "evidence" turned out to be illusory. Hence, Gettier proposed that a fourth condition be added, which together with the other three would be sufficient to guarantee knowledge: namely, that the justification be "indefeasible," that is, such that no other fact about the world would overturn or defeat it. Many think this a very tall order!

Whether or not the fourth condition is such as Gettier proposes is open to question since it may be too strong a requirement. Some modification, however, seems to be called for. (See Appendix I.)

The third objection rests on the observation that the *procedures* by which one would establish a proposition as true and those by which one would justify a belief are identical. Hence, it would be redundant to insist that a proposition be true as well as justified before one could claim to know it. Even if one admitted that "true" is a predicate of propositions, and "justified," a predicate of believers (i.e., believers are justified in holding their beliefs insofar as they have evidence), still, to be justified in holding a belief is precisely to have evidence for the truth of the proposition so believed. Evidence is sufficient when there are no more pertinent and relevant questions concerning the issue at hand. In a sense, then, the justification required by the proponents of this third objection must be "indefeasible" in Gettier's sense. Hence, in Gettier's counter-example, the justification is insufficient.

The fourth objection argues that knowledge is merely true belief and that no justification is either necessary or possible. This is much like the third objection, in that justification of a belief that is true is redundant (for the reason given under the third objection), or else incoherent, in that the justification would have to be known to be true and so itself require justification. This does not mean that justification has no place in human knowing; it means simply that knowing as such needs no justification, even if particular instances of it do.

True and False; Truth and Error

If "knowing" means justified true belief, it would be well to consider what is meant by "true." In the first place, "true" and "false" are properties of *propositions* only. Concepts are neither true nor false. They may perhaps be adequate or not, clear and distinct or not, but not true or false. Again, inferences are neither true nor false. They may be valid or invalid, sound or unsound, but not true or false.

In the second place, we are going to use "true" in the sense of "logical truth," as some philosophers have called it, or, perhaps better, in the sense of "epistemological truth." In general, this sense of the term indicates that the mind conforms to reality. It is distinguished from the sense of "ontological truth," in which reality conforms to the mind in the way in which an artifact conforms to the idea of it in the mind of its maker or in the way in which natural objects conform to the Divine Ideas in the Mind of the Creator. Aristotle defines the logically "true" as follows: a proposition is true if, of what is the case, it says that it is the case, or if, of what is not the case, it says that it is not the case. Otherwise, a proposition is false.[5] In more recent times, the logician Alfred

Tarski put Aristotle's insight in terms of "the semantic definition" of truth.[6] Take, for example, the proposition "Snow is white." It is true if and only if snow is white. This can be put schematically as follows:

"p" is T if and only if p.

This classical view of truth is sometimes called the correspondence theory.

In the Scholastic tradition both during the Middle Ages and in modern times the Aristotelian "correspondence" theory of truth was usually called the "conformity" theory and was usually expressed something like this: truth is the conformity of the mind to reality.[7] This formulation emphasizes the dominant role of the *object* in the truth relation. It stresses both the independence of truth from the acts of the individual minds by which it is grasped and the dominant role of the object in determining the mind. Expressed in this way, the theory is tied to the Aristotelian doctrine of matter and form (hence, the term "con*form*ity"), according to which physical objects are composed of two principles, prime matter and substantial form, of which only form is knowable by a process of abstraction. The form in the physical object and the form in the mind are identical, although the form's mode of existing in the mind and its mode of existing in the object are different. Hence, the mind "conforms" to reality.

It should be noted that "true" and "false" should not be confused with "affirmative" and "negative." Negative propositions can be true, and affirmative ones can be false. The truth or falsity of a proposition depends solely upon whether what it affirms or denies is the case in the world.

In the third place, truth and falsity are not synonyms for truth and error. Truth and falsity are properties of propositions, in the sense that a genuine proposition is *capable* of bearing just one of these values: true or false; truth and error are properties of assertions. Thus, for example, a proposition about something in the future may, at present, be neither true nor false but may take on one or the other of these values depending upon whether, and how, its truth conditions (actual events) turn out in the future. Again, it is entirely possible to be in error about a false proposition, namely, if one asserts it to be true. Similarly, one can be in error about a true proposition, namely, if one asserts it to be false. One has the truth about a true or a false proposition, respectively, if one asserts the one to be true and the other to be false. In a word, while truth and falsity are properties of propositions, truth and error are properties of the agent making the assertion and establish that agent to be "in truth" or "in error." Notice that although one can know that a certain proposition is false, one cannot knowingly be in error. For to know that one is in error is to have corrected the error, at least in the sense of refraining from making that judgment. Of course, one could knowingly propagate an error, but this would be a case of dissimulating (lying), not of judging.

Lastly, propositions admit neither degrees of truth nor changes in their truth value. A proposition cannot be a little bit true or mostly true. Either it is true or it is not, even if one cannot always tell in terms of the available evidence. Again, once the truth conditions for any proposition (affirmative or negative) have been fulfilled, its truth value cannot change with time. Thus, a proposition that is true at one time cannot become false at another.[8] These claims may at first seem strange or even just wrong, because we frequently speak of half-truths, or of approximations to the truth, or of truths that no longer hold. Yet upon closer examination it will be seen that these modes of common speech are either inaccurate or elliptical. For example, when we speak of a half-truth (say, "Gift-bearing Greeks are not to be trusted"), we do not mean that some "part" of the proposition is true, while some other "part" of it is false. We mean, rather, that a distinction is required for any claim about this matter to be true at all, and so, as it stands, the proposition is simply false. But to introduce a distinction is to replace the original proposition with one or more other propositions (say, "Some gift-bearing Greek in some circumstance or other is not to be trusted"—in fact, the Greek or Greeks who delivered the Trojan horse). In general, whenever a proposition requires a distinction in order to be true, that proposition as it stands is simply false and is to be replaced with a different proposition. Again, when we talk about truths' becoming false, we mean either that at some time in history people held a proposition to be true when in fact it was false, or that a proposition states a contingent historical event which happened at a certain place at a certain time and that events have since changed and so the proposition if uttered now about the present situation would be false. Yet again, we speak of future contingent acts (those which in fact will, but *need not*, happen), such as future free decisions or (if there are such things) future random occurrences. Propositions about them entertained *now*, that is, in the present, are as yet neither actually true nor actually false, even though they are *capable* of becoming either. Their truth conditions simply have not yet been met. Such propositions, therefore, can be *thought* about *now* but cannot be *known now*. Consider, for example, these two cases: (1) "The sun rotates about the earth," uttered by a medieval astronomer; (2) "Caesar is crossing the Rubicon," uttered by a Roman legionnaire marching with Caesar but now uttered by a twentieth-century tourist traveling in northern Italy. In the first case, the proposition did not *become* false, because it always was false. In the second, the proposition did not *become* false simply because it was uttered by a twentieth-century tourist. Rather, all the conditions for it to be true supposed by the speakers, namely, references to the date, are not explicitly stated. So, the modern tourist might have said truly that Caesar crossed the Rubicon in the first century B.C. Obviously, if the tourist asserted that Caesar is crossing the Rubicon *now*, the tourist is simply wrong (or perhaps joking?).

CERTITUDE

Properly speaking, certitude is an attribute of the person making an assertion. It measures the firmness of the person's assent to what he is affirming. We do sometimes talk of a proposition's being certain, but this simply means that the proposition is true and that there is enough evidence available to warrant a firm assent. Certitude, then, is a firm assent to a proposition. Certitude is warranted ("objective") if there is evidence known by (or at least available to) the person affirming the proposition sufficient to remove any reasonable doubt. Certitude is unwarranted (merely "subjective") if such evidence is lacking. It follows that certitude is no guarantee of truth. No matter how firmly convinced one may be of a proposition, unless there is evidence to support its truth, that conviction is merely subjective and therefore unwarranted. Warranted certitude, then, depends upon the truth of a proposition known as such through sufficient evidence.

Now, although "truth" and "falsity" do not admit of degrees, certitude does. Our conviction about, or assent to, a proposition can be more or less firm depending upon the evidence we have for it. Similarly, our certitude about a proposition can change in such a way that either what we formerly held as certain we now doubt or the converse. Notice, however, that if we say that a doubtful proposition has become certain or that a certain proposition has become doubtful, strictly speaking, we are talking, not about the *proposition*, but rather about our own grasp of the evidence.

Degrees of Certitude

Traditionally, the degrees of certitude were broken down as follows:[9]

1. Absolute or Metaphysical Certitude: all *possibility* of error is excluded, because denial of the proposition would involve a contradiction.

2. Physical Certitude: all *probability* of error is excluded, because the proposition's truth depends on the operation of a law of physical nature which, barring a miracle, necessitates the event enunciated in the proposition.

3. Moral Certitude: all *reasonable fear* of error is excluded, because the proposition's truth depends on a law of human behavior which, although it can be violated in a given case, is, in the absence of contrary evidence, presumed to be operative (e.g., "the bus driver will not attack me").

These divisions depend upon one's being able to establish the relevant generalizations about physical and human nature. They suppose that there are laws and that the laws are operating. If it should turn out that our claims about those laws are only probable, then, of course, judgments dependent upon them can be only probable. Most philosophers today would think that claims about physical and moral laws are only probable. Hence, it seems preferable to treat the matter as follows:

1. Certitude is absolute if the known evidence excludes the possibility of error. There are at least two cases. The first is that of analytically true propositions and principles the denial of which entails a logical contradiction. The second is that of synthetic and contingently true propositions whose denial involves a performatory (not a logical) contradiction. The best-known example of this second case is Descartes' "I think, therefore I am" (*"Cogito ergo sum"*).

2. Certitude is conditioned if the evidence that excludes the possibility of error includes certain conditions that are known to be fulfilled. An example is certitude about some contingent matter of fact. Some contingent matters of fact can be denied without either a logical or a performatory contradiction. Yet, if I know the conditions under which such a proposition would be true, and if I know that in fact those conditions are fulfilled, then I know that the proposition is true because I have grasped it as virtually unconditioned.

3. A judgment is probable if there is some evidence to support it but not enough to render it virtually unconditioned. In such cases there are relevant and pertinent questions still to be answered concerning the matter at hand. Probable judgments are the object of well-founded opinion. An opinion is well founded when it is not a mere guess. Strictly speaking, all scientific judgments are of this sort.

Evidence: The Criterion of Truth and the Motive of Certitude

Our discussion of truth and certitude implied a notion of evidence. The word "evidence" comes from the Latin *"videre"* (to see) and *"e"* (which has the sense of arising from or separated from and is variously translated as "from," "away," or "out of"). The Latin word *"evidens"* came to mean "plain," "clear," or "manifest." Evidence, then, is what makes a proposition plain, clear, or manifest.

We may take evidence to mean whatever supports the truth of a claim. In general, evidence for a proposition is a condition or set of conditions which, if fulfilled, implies the truth of that proposition.[10] Evidence may be sufficient (adequate) or not (inadequate). Evidence is insufficient or inadequate if it is only a *necessary* (but not a sufficient) condition for the truth of the proposition in question. In such a case, the evidence is something without which the proposition in question would not be true. Inductive support for an hypothesis is usually of this sort, and it can be put schematically like this in an *invalid* conditional syllogism:

>If p, then q
>But q
>Therefore (probably) p.

q is evidence for p, but it is only a necessary condition for p's truth. It is not sufficient. Hence, we conclude "probably p." Still, if q were false, so would p be. If this is not immediately clear to you, substitute for p and q "it is raining" and "the streets are wet." Then, of course, if it is raining, the streets are wet; but even if the streets are wet, we can conclude only that it is likely that it has been raining since the streets might be wet because someone hosed them down. Still, if the streets are bone dry, then it cannot be raining:

>If p, then q
>But not q
>Therefore (certainly) not p.

Evidence is sufficient or adequate if the fulfillment of the condition implies (and, hence, is sufficient for) the truth of the proposition for which it is evidence. When evidence is sufficient, the proposition which it supports can be asserted as detached from the evidence once the evidential conditions are known to be fulfilled. Such a proposition is said to be *virtually unconditioned*. (A proposition would be *formally unconditioned* if had no conditions, that is, if it depended on nothing else for its truth.)

Odds and Ends

Ignorance is simply the absence of knowledge. If ignorance were total, no questions could arise, no answers be given, and no errors made. *Opinion* is a hesitant assent to a proposition. There is evidence but it is not sufficient. *Belief* is a firm conviction or assent. Knowledge, then, is a special case of belief, namely, where one has evidence sufficient to justify the belief. Religious belief is another special case, namely, where one does not have direct evidence sufficient to justify the belief. One may, and perhaps should, have indirect evidence sufficient to render the belief reasonable (that is, to render the act of believing a reasonable thing to do). This might be in the form of evidence concerning the credibility of a witness testifying to a religious truth. Finally, *doubt* is the suspension of assent because evidence either is entirely lacking or is too weak to make other choices less likely.

Notes

1. *Theaetetus*, 201-10; *Republic*, 509D-11E.

2. A. D. Woolzey ("Are Propositions Eternal Entities in Some Platonic Realm?" in *Theory of Knowledge* [London: Hutchinson University Library, 1962], pp. 102-21) argues that there is no need so to think of them. But see R. Bradley and N. Swartz, *Possible Worlds: An Introduction to Logic and Its Philosophy* (Indianapolis and Cambridge: Hackett, 1963), pp. 121-23.

3. See W. V. Quine, "Paradox," in *Mathematics in the Modern World: Readings from the* SCIENTIFIC AMERICAN (San Francisco and London: Freeman, 1968), pp. 200-208. See also his *From a Logical Point of View*, 2nd rev. ed. (New York: Harper Torchbooks, 1963), pp. 130-38.

4. For the first challenge, see K. Lehrer, "Belief and Knowledge," *Philosophical Review*, 77 (1968). 491-99; J. Harrison, "Does Knowing Imply Believing?" *Philosophical Quarterly*, 15 (1963), 322-32; and C. Black, "Knowledge Without Belief," *Analysis*, 31 (1970-1971), 153-58.

For the second challenge, see E. Gettier, "Is Justified True Belief Knowledge?" *Analysis*, 23 (1963), 121-23; K. Lehrer, "Knowledge, Truth, and Evidence," ibid., 25 (1965), 168-76. For a complete survey of the controversy created by Gettier, see R. K. Shope, *The Analysis of Knowing: A Decade of Research* (Princeton: Princeton University Press, 1983). The simplified version of the "paradox" used in our text is from Bradley and Swartz, *Possible Worlds*, pp. 126-27.

For the third challenge, see J. H. Gill, "Knowledge Is Justified Belief: Period," *International Philosophical Quarterly*, 35, No. 4 (December 1985), 381-91.

For the fourth challenge, see Crispin Sartwell, "Why Knowledge Is

Merely True Belief," *Journal of Philosophy*, 89 (1992), 167-80.

5. *Metaphysics*, 1011B25-30.

6. Alfred Tarski, "The Semantic Conception of Truth," *Philosophy and Phenomenological Research*, 4 (1944), 341-76, reprinted in *Readings in Philosophical Analysis*, edd. Herbert Feigl and Wilfred Sellars (New York: Appleton-Century-Crofts, 1949), pp. 52-84.

7. See, e.g., R. F. O'Neill, S.J., *Theories of Knowledge* (Englewood Cliffs, N.J.: Prentice-Hall, 1960), pp. 62-68.

8. See, e.g., Alan R. White, *Truth* (Garden City, N.Y.: Doubleday Anchor, 1970), passim, for a discussion of whether truth changes or admits of degrees.

9. See, e.g. O'Neill, *Theories of Knowledge*, pp. 102-11.

10. Bernard J. F. Lonergan, S.J., *Insight: A Study in Human Understanding* (New York: Philosophical Library, 1956), esp. chap. 10, "Reflective Understanding," pp. 279-316.

STUDY QUESTIONS

1. What in general is the "philosophy of knowledge" trying to establish?

2. Why cannot one meaningfully pose the question "Do I know anything at all?" Explain.

3. Give some of the more common meanings of the term "to know." In what sense are we using it?

4. How would you characterize "proposition" according to the values "true" and "false"?

5. How would you characterize a proposition that is neither true nor false? Why? Give an example.

6. Distinguish "proposition" from "judgment." Why is it that only in judgment is there "knowing" in our sense of the term?

7. How did Plato distinguish knowledge from true belief?

8. What is Gettier's paradox, and what are we to think of it?

9. Is it accurate to speak of concepts as true or false? Inferences? Explain.

10. What is meant by "logical (epistemological) truth"? How did Tarski try to formulate it?

11. Distinguish "truth and falsity" from "truth and error." How are these pairs related?

12. Discuss the oft-heard claims (1) that a proposition is more or less true (false) and (2) that the truth value of a proposition can change.

13. What is meant by "certitude"? When is it objective?

14. Does certitude admit of degrees? Explain.
15. Explain the traditional division of certitude.
16. What is the chief weakness in this way of looking at certitude?
17. What is meant by "absolute certitude"? Explain each of the two cases which fall under it.
18. What is meant by "conditioned certitude"? How does "the grasp of the virtually unconditioned" apply here?
19. What is meant by saying that a judgment is probable?
20. Explain the derivation and current meaning of the term "evidence."
21. When is evidence "necessary"? When is it "sufficient"?
22. Illustrate sufficient evidence using the conditional syllogism.
23. Distinguish "formally unconditioned" from "virtually unconditioned." How does this relate to sufficient evidence?
24. Define the following: Ignorance, Opinion, Belief, Doubt.

1

Skepticism

WHAT HAS PRINCIPALLY MOTIVATED philosophers to inquire into the nature and extent of human knowing is the *fact of error*. On the one hand, they looked upon the fact of error as scandalous. How could it be that in matters of importance, sometimes of vital importance, we make mistakes—frequently despite our best efforts? On the other hand, they looked upon error as puzzling—even mysterious. How is it possible for the careful inquirer to err when, after all, either he has sufficient evidence or he does not and so in the first case knows that he has the truth and in the second knows that he does not yet know?

Add to the fact of error the equally disconcerting fact that even "experts" frequently disagree on what the truth is. How can it be that intelligent and well-trained people frequently hold not only different but incompatible views? This is true even in the hard sciences where one would expect greater objectivity and detachment from self-interest. Surely this demands some explanation.

Again, philosophers have been struck by the apparent discrepancy between the scientific and the common-sense views of the world. Thus, the physicist Eddington asked which of the two tables—the solid, colored, impenetrable table of sense experience or the swirling cloud of particles in an energy field as understood by science—is real.[1] Wilfrid Sellars thinks that the scientific image is the really real world (the noumenon), while the manifest image is only appearance (the phenomenon).[2]

These and other curiosities about human claims to know the world have raised questions, not to say doubts, in the minds of many reflective people. To have doubts about a truth-claim is to be skeptical. The ancient Greek philosophers had already been puzzled by peculiar sense experiences, like illusions, dreams, or hallucinations, which sometimes were difficult, if not impossible, to distinguish from "normal," veridical perceptions of physical objects. These statistically unusual experiences raised questions in their minds about the reliability of perception and so raised doubts about the perceptual experiences that most people simply took for granted. These thinkers would not be impressed by "seeing is believing." In fact, they would consider seeing as a weak guarantee indeed of the reality of what is seen. It is to throw light on these puzzles that we undertake our present inquiry. It is to help us distinguish legitimate from illegitimate doubt.

Never to doubt anything is naïve. Always to doubt everything is impossible. Intelligence, therefore, demands that we be critical, in the sense that we look for evidence for our opinions, beliefs, and claims to knowledge. Insofar as evidence is lacking or is insufficient, we may legitimately doubt. Perhaps more accurately put: doubt is legitimate when there is reason to doubt.

Absolute Skepticism

The term "skepticism" is derived from the Greek word *"skeptomai"* (Greek), meaning in the first place "I consider carefully" or "I look carefully" and in a derived sense "I doubt." Certain ancient Greek philosophers were called "skeptics" because they questioned things and brought into doubt many things that ordinary people simply took for granted. Among them are usually counted Pyrrho (ca. 360–270 B.C.), Carneades (ca. 214–129 B.C.), and Sextus Empiricus (ca. A.D. 250). These thinkers pushed their doubts so far as to give the impression at least that they doubted absolutely everything. Such an extreme position came to be known as *universal* (or absolute) *skepticism*.[3] It amounts to complete intellectual despair, and our first project is to show that such a position is untenable.

The point here is not whether in fact any of the above-named philosophers (or any other philosopher for that matter) ever held complete skepticism. It is, rather, to show that such a position both defeats itself and is defeated by evident fact. Our attack on this position, then, is twofold: (1) negatively, it will be shown that absolute skepticism is internally incoherent, and (2) positively, certain facts will be adduced which literally *cannot* be doubted because of the evidence.

Consider, then, what absolute skepticism proposes: it claims that no proposition whatsoever can be known to be true. This, in effect, is to deny that we can know anything at all. Sometimes it is put as a denial of truth. A question naturally arises concerning the status of skepticism itself as a claim about the human condition. Can it be known to be true? Is it itself a truth? One can easily see that no coherent answer is possible. If one answers "yes," the original claim is denied. If one answers "no," the original claim is again denied. In effect, the only consistent thing an absolute skeptic can do is to keep silent altogether. As soon as he opens his mouth in speech, he has refuted himself.

Notice that in a sense it is useless to argue with an absolute skeptic since he simply will not admit any argument as sound precisely because he will admit no proposition as certainly true. But, then, no such argument is really necessary since the internal incoherence of absolute skepticism already defeats it. If one insists on holding it (presumably as true!), then one is faced no longer with an intellectual problem but with an emotional one.

The problem, of course, lies in the fact that absolute skepticism refers to itself. As an assertion of a position, it affirms its own truth and hence denies the absolute universality of the skeptical position. One might try to fix this up by excepting from doubt the skeptical position. But then the camel's nose is under the tent, because one would have admitted the mind's *capacity* to know the truth, and all the old questions concerning sufficient evidence in various cases return. One might hedge about absolute skepticism, saying that one does not know whether it is true or not, but then, of course, the question arises about whether one knows that one doubts it.

Perhaps the best-known attempt to refute skepticism positively, that is, by adducing a matter of fact which is so evidently true that it cannot be doubted, is that of Descartes (1596-1650).[4] Descartes proposed a new *Method* of reasoning which would guarantee that one reach the truth. The first rule of that method was to consider as *false* any proposition about which there could possibly be the slightest doubt. The "methodic doubt" is sometimes called exaggerated or hyperbolic. Descartes went so far as to suppose an "evil genius" who continually deceives us in all our ordinary judgments. The point of this "super-doubt" was to produce at least one proposition concerning a matter of existential and contingent fact which cannot possibly be denied. With this one solid piece of ground on which, like Archimedes, to put his feet, Descartes would reconstruct human knowledge beyond all skeptical doubt. Of course, this one indubitable truth that Descartes discovered was his *"Cogito ergo sum"* ("I think, therefore I am").

What makes the *Cogito* indubitable is that the evidence for it is not some abstract truth but an *action*, a *doing* by the one uttering the judgment. The very act of making the judgment is evidence for the existence of the one judging. Perhaps another way to get at the force of the *Cogito* is to try to deny your own existence. No doubt, you can speak the words "I do not exist," but you cannot *assert* it precisely because the act of assertion itself (a form of Descartes' *Cogito*) makes your own existence evident. Some philosophers have given the reason why one cannot deny one's own existence a name: a *performatory* contradiction.[5] They mean to distinguish this sort of contradiction from a purely *logical* contradiction. The opposite of a logical contradiction is a tautology, that is, a proposition that is true by virtue of its semantic and/or syntactic structure. Such a proposition is always and everywhere true—necessarily true—it could not be not true. Now, this does not quite fit the assertion "I exist," since such a proposition, uttered in a definite historical context, is not a tautology; it is not necessarily true. After all, I do not exist necessarily; there was a time when I did not exist and there will be a time when I will no longer exist (at least in the same way as I do now). "I exist" is a contingently true statement of fact. Its truth, therefore, is conditioned, but those very conditions are known by the asserter to be fulfilled in the very act of assertion (since that act manifests their fulfillment). Hence, denial of one's existence is contradicted by the very performance—the act of denial.

Two remarks are perhaps in order before we leave Descartes' *Cogito*. (1) Descartes was not the first one to have discovered this sort of argument against absolute skepticism. In the fifth century St. Augustine proposed a similar argument (*City of God* 2.26). Augustine put it this way: *"Si fallor, sum"* ("If I err, I exist"). Augustine's point is the same as Descartes', and the force of his argument is the same: namely, the very act of making a mistake asserts the agent's existence. (2) Before coming upon the *Cogito*,

Descartes admitted that mathematical truths were indubitable. Why was this not enough to overcome skepticism? The reason is that mathematical truths are not existential; that is, they do not, *of themselves*, tell us anything about the existing world. Mathematics deals with *possible* ways in which space might be organized. It does not tell us either that there is any real space or how that space is in fact organized. We might put it this way: mathematics deals with thinking possible patterns, not with knowing any actual ones. Descartes wanted to have certain, indubitable knowledge about the actual, existing world. Hence, the peculiar importance for him of the *Cogito*.

At this point one very important conclusion can be drawn: the human mind *is* capable of knowing; it is capable of grasping the truth; it is capable of certitude. All that remains is to explore the nature and scope of that capacity.

Subjectivism

Many post-Cartesian philosophers have assumed that the *only* thing we can know with certitude is ourselves and our conscious acts. More accurately put perhaps: these philosophers claim that this is all we can know *directly*. All claims about the non-self, the non-ego, are in themselves subject to doubt. If knowledge of them is to be justified at all, it must be done by some argument or inference. In a word, knowledge of the non-self (if there is any) is indirect. Thus arose what is known as "the problem of the bridge." How does one "get outside" the mind to the "external" or "objective" world of the non-ego?

Ironically, Descartes' vigorous attempt to refute skepticism once for all is largely responsible for this "subjectivist" turn in philosophy. Why he could not doubt the *Cogito*, Descartes thought, was that, by his reason, he clearly and distinctly apprehended himself as a thinking thing (*res cogitans*). From this he concluded that whatever he apprehended clearly and distinctly by reason was true. Out of this came the "clear and distinct idea" as the criterion of truth. But this implied that *what is known* is the clear and distinct *idea*. It further implied that what is distinctly and clearly apprehended is *self-authenticating*; that is, it carries its own guarantee of truth.

If we add to this the distrust that Descartes had of the senses, the problem of the bridge is not far off. For Descartes all reports of the "external world" delivered to us by the senses were open to doubt. In the first place, the senses are notoriously deceptive, and, in the second place, all the data of sense could be produced directly in our consciousness by God without any need for an "external world" at all. At least such a position is not self-contradictory, and so it is possible to doubt that the senses are a source of knowledge about a world outside of us. In a word, the senses, unlike reason, do not carry their own guarantee of truth. They are not self-authenticating sources of knowledge. In fact, Descartes did rehabilitate the senses indirectly. He did so by appealing to the truthfulness of God. After all, Descartes reasoned, God created our senses and He put in us our common-sense conviction about the external world. But God would not deceive us in this matter. Hence, according to Descartes, the basis of trust in the senses as delivering knowledge of the physical world is the veracity of God.

We will show that such a roundabout route is entirely unnecessary. There is direct evidence sufficient to support our conviction that there is a world other than the self of which we have some certain knowledge. In fact, there is as much evidence for the reality of the non-ego as there is for the ego.

As a first step in establishing such knowledge, consider the pairs of terms "subjective/objective," "internal/external," "self/non-self." They are correlatives; that is, they have meaning only in reference to each other. Consequently, for the problem of subjectivism to arise in the first place, I have to know what the term means; but for me to know this, I have to know what its correlate means. I must, then, have a perspective that is beyond both of them. In the act of knowing, I must be beyond subjective/objective, inside/outside. I recognize them as distinctions *within* my act of knowing. Hence, if subjectivism's claim were correct (namely, that I know *nothing but* the self and its acts), I could never raise the question of whether there were anything else that is "objective" or "outside." It would simply never occur to me. I would be in Hegel's moonless night in which all the cows are black. So, the very fact that the question is raised means that it has been answered in a general way. There *is* indeed a non-ego of some sort.

Again, consider what the subjectivist's claim might mean: perhaps that knowledge is *exclusively* constituted by the subject—as it were "out of whole cloth." There would be no role for the object to play in knowing. The object does not determine what is known; the subject determines how things are thought to be. In the limit case, then, things would be just as the subject thinks they are, because nothing would have any reality independently of being thought by the subject. Such an extreme position is called *solipsism* (from the Latin *solus ipse*, meaning "he himself alone"). To reduce a philosophical position to solipsism is generally considered to have reduced it to an absurdity. The philosophical joke goes that the solipsist wrote a book defending his position!

The subjectivist's claim might mean simply that the subject plays an active role in knowing, that the subject is not just a passive spectator who receives knowledge from an object. Not only does knowing involve a subject but it also is an act of a subject. The subject actively uses its capacity or power to know and so to that extent brings something to the knowing relation. This does not exclude the role of the object or diminish its importance and even dominance in some ways. It simply indicates that there is no knowledge until the subject reacts to or interacts with the object. In this sense, of course, subjectivism is unobjectionable, but the precise role of subject and object in knowing would have to be carefully determined.

Let us now consider what evidence there is that we know the world of the non-ego. The only possible place to look for such evidence is in an act of what appears to be clear and evident knowledge of the extra-mental world. We must then critically reflect upon the case to see whether we can make explicit what it implicitly contains. Let us choose the common and very concrete experience of holding a conversation with someone, the case of person-to-person *dialogue*.[6] Let us suppose that this situation involves an exchange of significant questions and answers, that I ask questions to which I do not know the answers, that in the course of the conversation I receive answers that correspond precisely to my questions, and, finally, that I observe carefully the actions and gestures of the other party.

The first thing to remark about this common experience is that it involves action—a doing—in which the knower is engaged, both in the sense of determining the course of the conversation and in the sense of being determined by it. Second, this interaction seems to be spontaneous and free on the part of the participants, because neither can predict, project, or deduce what the other will ask or respond. Each awaits the response of the other; each learns from the other's response. Each is informed by the other and hence is changed—is acted upon. But action is the sure sign of reality, of existence.

No doubt, the experience of dialogue is only one of several common experiences that give evidence of the real existence of the non-ego. Perhaps in some ways it is the most convincing because one easily recognizes in the responses and behavior of one's partner responses like one's own human responses and behavior. But any situation in which I seem to be actively engaged with something that resists, confronts, or otherwise eludes my control will do. I would suppose that getting one's hand caught in the car door would be convincing evidence of an external world!

Furthermore, there is good experimental evidence that one does not come to an explicit awareness of oneself as an existing individual except through interaction with the non-self.[7] This would mean, not that we have direct intuition of ourselves in a clear and distinct idea, as Descartes thought, but rather that we gradually, through the experience of struggle and resistance, become aware of ourselves as distinct from other items of which we are conscious. Thus, it seems that the newborn does not at first distinguish itself from its environment. It seems to take everything to be an extension of itself, or to be continuous with itself. Only when its needs, wants, and desires are frustrated does it begin to recognize that the environment is distinct from and over against it. By the experience of such frustration and dependence it begins to recognize that its own body is not just like any other object in its experience but rather has a very special relation to its awareness. Thus, recognition of the self as self depends on our experiences of our own ignorance, of our dependence, and of our errors.

So far, then, we have found that neither absolute skepticism nor radical subjectivism is tenable. The human mind, therefore, can know something. At the very least, we each know beyond any possible doubt that we exist. Beyond that, however, and correlative to it, we have numerous common experiences which testify with compelling force that we also know the existence of an external world (a non-ego). Furthermore, we know something about the external world inasmuch as it acts upon us in particular ways. Thus, I know that the non-ego with which I am engaged in dialogue is a being like myself, in that it manifests rational behavior (answering my questions).

These considerations show us the presence in our knowing experience of evidence, truth, and certitude. Evidence is at work because something has become manifest to us. Truth is present because through evidence we have grasped the virtually unconditioned. The truth thus grasped renders our judgment of the matter beyond doubt, and so we have warranted certitude.

Value-Skepticism

Besides absolute skepticism and radical subjectivism, some philosophers have held a restricted or mitigated skepticism. Consider what is called "value-skepticism." This position makes a sharp distinction between factual claims and evaluative judgments. This distinction is intended to show a real *dichotomy* between fact and value. This was first made popular by Hume when he asserted that there is not, and there cannot be, any logical connection between what is the case and what ought to be the case.[8] Following Hume, many philosophers not only distinguish fact and value but separate them by an unbridgeable gap. Factual judgments and value judgments are of such radically different kinds, according to these thinkers, that they can have no logical bearing on each another. Hence, no factual claim can serve as evidence for an evaluative claim; no evaluative claim can in any way modify the facts of the case.

The so-called fact/value dichotomy is usually interpreted to mean that *only* factual claims can be cognitive. Evaluative claims, by their very nature, cannot be. Such a view is based on an epistemological theory according to which (1) we can *know* only facts,

(2) a "fact" is whatever *is* the case, and (3) "what is the case" is the directly or indirectly observable and, therefore, verifiable. But value-claims cannot be "observed." Hence, they are not among the "facts" and so cannot be "known." This sort of account of knowing is typical of positivism and certain forms of empiricism.

There has been a variety of opinion as to what evaluative claims are, if they are not cognitive.[9] The responses differ according to the kind of empiricism a philosopher holds. In general, proponents of the fact/value dichotomy are either "hard" or "soft" empiricists. The hardness or softness of their empiricism is a function of what they require for verification. "Soft" empiricists ease the requirement by allowing "verifiable in principle" instead of insisting upon actual verification. "Hard" empiricists usually insist that value and ethical claims cannot be affirmed at all and any attempt to do so is just an abuse of both thought and language. "Soft" empiricists might tolerate the popular use of "judgment" as applied to value-claims, but they immediately translate those "judgments" into some other kind of utterance. Some have said that they are merely expressions of emotion. Others translate them into exhortations or even commands ("go thou and do likewise"; "don't do that!"). In any case, both hard and soft empiricists generally agree that they are not knowledge of the world. To repeat: knowledge of the world is confined exclusively to fact, where fact is understood to be what can be observed by the senses. The empiricist and positivist presupposition concerning knowing comes down to this: knowing is "taking a look."

On this view, then, one must hold a radical skepticism with respect to values since no amount of knowledge concerning the world can ever decide which values are to be held.

Oddly enough, such skepticism concerning values is often linked with a skepticism concerning fact as well. The reason for this is not that, in principle, facts cannot be known, but rather that there is some fault in the theory of how facts are known, and this fault ultimately calls into doubt the very possibility of such knowledge. This is to say that frequently empiricist and/or positivist theories of knowledge imply skepticism because of a mistaken presupposition about the very act of knowing. It remains to be seen, of course, whether such empiricist/positivist theories of knowledge can be remedied without at the same time removing what makes them empiricist or positivist in any interesting sense.

Perhaps an illustration of such implicit skepticism would help. Take Hume, for example. He *assumes* that the basic unit in human knowing is the sense impression. Furthermore, he is careful to warn us not to suppose that such impressions are *impressions* coming from the "outside." He declares that we do not, and cannot, know that. Hence, like Locke, he assumes that what one knows are one's ideas and not things through one's ideas. Hence, the "problem of the bridge" (how to get outside of consciousness), and, hence, the absolute skepticism consequent upon another radical subjectivism.

Those who would follow the Locke–Hume analysis of knowing must come to skepticism of both value and fact, that is, to absolute skepticism. Many would hold that empiricism does not commit them to such an outcome and, hence, that they can correct Locke–Hume. The question, then, seems to be: In what way does modern empiricism make an interesting alternative to the realism of Aristotle and the medieval philosophers according to which we know the external world with certitude at least in some instances?

The fact/value dichotomy held out the hope that there is a value-free, value-neutral, science(s) which would have absolute authority because it is totally "objective." So the social sciences, for example, claimed (and, in some circles, still do claim) a special importance in the reasonable ordering of society because they are free of the particular emotive bias of this or that value-system. Thus, for example, it was hoped that an entire system of public education could be built upon these sciences, an education that would be free of subjective prejudice and predilection. Unfortunately for that sort of enterprise, the fact/value dichotomy has come in for severe criticism, such that it seems to many to have broken down completely—not in the sense that fact and value cannot be distinguished, but in the sense that they cannot be separated.

A great deal might be said in criticism of value-skepticism. In fact, the latter half of the twentieth century has seen an effort by philosophers (even by those sympathetic to empiricism) to put reason back into ethics.[10] One of the problems with value-skepticism (besides its being founded on a faulty understanding of cognition) is that, like absolute skepticism and radical subjectivism, it is self-referentially inconsistent. Scientists themselves remark often enough that science can be pursued only by those who love the truth. And, hence, the very motive force behind the position is the love of truth and of scientific "objectivity." Of course, these loves are authentic; they are true values. Hence, the expression of those values is an expression of truth. If it were not, there would be no good reason to hold such a position. It would be merely arbitrary. Hence, value-skepticism must be rejected, and some account must be given of human knowing which will allow a connection between fact and value without at the same time destroying their distinction.

Relativism

Absolute skepticism and radical subjectivism are extreme positions that are easily enough shown to be untenable. Sometimes, however, these positions are disguised in more popular forms that make their absurdity more difficult to discern and so make them more acceptable. These covert forms of skepticism and subjectivism go under the collective name of relativism.[11]

Relativism is attractive to many for several reasons, not the least of which is that there is something right about it. It is the case that many of our judgments are relative to personal taste, to a particular context, or to a certain cultural environment. Furthermore, an easy-going relativism seems a way to avoid what might be unpleasant confrontation. It can be a way to put off hard questions that risk disturbing the peace. So "live and let live" might be relativism's advice; after all, beauty is in the eye of the beholder. Everyone knows that when in Rome one should do as the Romans do. All these familiar saws support relativism in one way or another. Finally, in a pluralistic society such as ours, not only is it socially acceptable to adopt such an attitude, but not doing so might well be politically dangerous. At the very least, insisting on the universality and objectivity of truth is not calculated to win popularity.

In general, relativism denies that there is any universal and objective truth. In one rather crude form it holds that truth is whatever the individual believes. Usually this form of relativism is restricted by its adherents to moral, religious, and value judgments. A more sophisticated version claims that all truth is contextual and perspectival. Truth depends upon one's point of view and upon one's presuppositions. The most complex position is cultural relativism. Truth depends upon an entire world-view defined and inculcated by society in terms of its culture. So all-pervasive and so subtle is this cultural brainwashing that it frequently goes undetected by those whom it affects.

Correctly relativism opposes the extremely rationalistic attitude which exaggerates the power of the human intellect. Relativism more often than not is connected with empiricism and thus, correctly again, stresses the role of sense experience in human knowing. Again, relativism rightly points out the role of environment in what human beings come to believe.

Yet, for all that, relativism is fatally flawed in several ways. In the first place, insofar as it is self-referential, it is inconsistent. Concerning itself, relativism must be making an absolute claim or no claim at all. Hence, at least one truth-claim is independent and universal. In the second place, relativism can be reduced to absolute skepticism or to subjectivism. Behind relativism is the conviction that we cannot know reality as it is in itself. All that is available to us is appearance; but since appearance can be deceptive, all knowledge claims are suspect. The subject cannot "know" reality without altering it according to the subject's capacity. Hence, "truth" is relative to the subject. The subject, in effect, becomes the measure of truth. Truth becomes what the subject believes. Reality becomes what those beliefs assert. In any case, relativism takes away objectivity and universality from truth and thus evacuates its meaning.

Finally, relativism supposes that truth is relative to something or other and that the something or other can itself be known and so can be the subject of true judgments. But, then, whatever is chosen as the standard (oneself, some context, or some cultural environment) must be known independently of that standard. Thus, if I claim, for example, that some proposition p is true from a certain perspective or in a certain context, I have to know the perspective or the context. But this knowledge cannot be in terms of the perspective or context in question; nor can it be in terms of some other perspective or context since this would lead to an infinite regress. There must be at least something common to all perspectives and contexts which makes them such and by which I recognize them for what they are.

Part of the problem in dealing intelligently with relativism is a confusion between relativity and relativism. Recognizing relativity in knowledge merely implies that knowledge is relational, and this recognition is compatible with the claim that some knowledge is objective and universal. A typical example is observation reports made by scientists using different frames of reference. Their reports of the same physical event would be different (because the frames of reference are different), but the truth about the physical event they are reporting could be the same (hence, objective with respect to the observers) if one report can be translated into the other by means of transformation rules. The objective content of such reports, then, is what remains invariant under framework transformation. Hence, Einstein's theory of relativity does not support relativism; on the contrary, it stoutly denies it.

Postmodernism and Deconstructionism

The latest version of relativism has been given the name "postmodernism" presumably because "modernism" or "modern philosophy" has been declared dead and been superseded by a new skepticism. The "modern philosophy" which postmodernism supplants seems to be any that gives a predominant role to reason whether that be understood after the manner of the Empiricists or the Rationalists of the Enlightenment period of Western thought. This emphasis upon reason was further developed by nineteenth-century Idealism especially among the German philosophers. Of course, there had always been voices objecting to the exaggerated role given to reason by modern philosophy. We need only think of Kierkegaard and the entire Existentialist movement on the Continent and the linguistic analysts in England during the first half of the twentieth century.

The British linguistic analysts had in common a rejection of German Idealism, especially in its Hegelian form. But beyond this opposition to continental Rationalism, the analysts had little in common except to give philosophy a "linguistic turn." This amounted to the claim that analysis of ordinary language would show the metaphysics of Idealism to be wrong. G. E. Moore, for example, was convinced that such an analysis would show that common-sense realism is justified. Bertrand Russell held that a logical analysis of language would yield the ontological structure of being (a position called Logical Atomism). This isomorphism of linguistic and ontological structures would thus provide a grounding for knowledge without recourse to "metaphysical" entities. Finally, Ludwig Wittgenstein tried to show that all philosophical problems are pseudo-problems because they are due to a failure rightly to understand language. Rather than solve such puzzles, philosophers are to dissolve them by language analysis. Once this is done, we will see the world aright.

The postmodernists, however, seem to draw their agenda and their inspiration from Nietzsche and to give philosophy, not a linguistic turn, but more properly a turn to linguistics.[12] Nietzsche's biting criticism of Enlightenment and of post-Enlightenment Idealism (Fichte, Schelling, Hegel) led the way to the "death of God" both culturally (the Christian influence on European culture was waning) and philosophically (the very concept of God was no longer considered worthy of serious consideration) and to the "Will to Power" as the very essence of mankind.

The Nietzchean attack tried to show that any attempt to reach objective truth (say, through metaphysical analysis) is illusory and, hence, that the operative force in culture is not Truth, but Power. Hence, in the end, philosophy is politics—the imposition of one's opinions and values by persuasion if possible, by force if necessary.

This postmodern retreat from truth and from metaphysics opened the way for the triumph of rhetoric over logic. This "turn to linguistics" began with a movement called Structuralism made popular by Claude Lévi-Strauss.[13] A major point made by structuralists which fostered the new skepticism and relativism was the claim that "social structures"—defined as a set of key and stable relationships which set up the juridical and cultural ties between individual members in a particular society—are not "out there" in the world but are only a model in the human mind. The paradigm is that of signified (model in the mind) and signifier (observable components of a particular culture). Hence, these social structures are relative and conventional, if not arbitrary. Several philosophers have pushed the sign-signified model of human awareness and knowledge to the point of linguistic idealism: there is no reality knowable by us except the linguistic signs themselves. On such a view, the signs do not "stand for" something else known through them but are themselves what is known.

An extreme example of this "turn to linguistics" is "deconstructionism." (See Appendix IV.) The deconstructionists, like Nietzsche, aim to discredit Western philosophy's "logocentrism" by showing the inadequacy of any linguistic/conceptual framework (social structure?) for capturing the real and reducing it to a set of universal principles and laws. The tactic employed is to take apart (to deconstruct) philosophical claims to systematic completeness, showing the weaknesses and inadequacies of each. There is a strong and a weak form of this deconstruction. The weak or soft form is nothing but a warning against the limitations of language and of conceptual schemes in representing reality. This form neither destroys rationality nor despairs of understanding the real, even if the understanding is always inadequate. The strong form, however, would destroy all rational discourse, whether philosophical or literary, since it maintains that the contextual nature and inevitable vagueness of linguistic signs make them always infected with a certain ambiguity that makes definitive interpretation impossible. Hence, the connection between sign and signified is not so certain as one might have believed. Since sign and signified define the reality of both social structure and cultural milieu, the "reality" of each is always ambiguous and open to endless reinterpretation. Hence, there is no "truth" that transcends the individuals who interpret any particular culture.

Some of the major figures in postmodern deconstruction are the French philosophers Jacques Derrida and Jean-François Lyotard. In the United States Richard Rorty has espoused a kindred position.[14]

Some critical evaluation of the deconstructionist enterprise is in order. Like other forms of relativism and skepticism it falls into a self-referential fallacy. In its strong form, at least, when deconstruction denies any firm connection between sign and signified, between language and reality, it renders its own utterances meaningless and thus incapable of any judgment concerning the truth of its own claims. Some might try to make light of this objection by recourse to the "playfulness" of reason which does not take anything seriously, not even its own critique. But, of course, that will not do since the game itself is self-defeating, if it can be played at all. On the other hand, in its weak or soft form, deconstructive techniques can serve the useful and salutary purpose of warning against the pretensions of Enlightenment's reason.

Our initial conclusions about human knowledge are modest but important. Absolute skepticism, radical subjectivism, and various forms of relativism are untenable. This does not mean that one should never be "skeptical," that is, doubt this or that claim, whether factual or evaluative. Nor does this mean that the subject contributes nothing to knowledge, since the structure of knowing is a relation between knowing subject and object known. It simply means that as general accounts of human knowing those positions break down. Positively, one can conclude that the human mind is capable of knowing something and that some truth-claims are objective and universal. What those claims are and under what conditions they can be made remain to be examined, even though the astute reader can already make a partial list.

Notes

1. A. Eddington, *The Nature of the Physical World* (Cambridge: Cambridge University Press, 1928), pp. xi–xii.

2. Wilfrid Sellars, "Philosophy and the Scientific Image of Man," *Science, Perception and Reality* (London: Routledge & Kegan Paul, 1963), pp. 1–40.

3. See R. H. Popkin, *The History of Skepticism from Erasmus to Descartes* (Assen, The Netherlands: Van Gorcum, 1960), for the revival of Greek skepticism in the sixteenth century. For a sympathetic account of ancient Greek skepticism, see Leo Groarke, *Greek Skepticism: Anti-Realist Trends in Ancient Thought* (Montreal & Kingston: McGill-Queen's, 1990).

4. See Descartes, *Discourse on Method* and *Meditations*, in *The*

Philosophical Works of Descartes I, edd. E. S. Haldane & G. R. T. Ross (New York: Dover, 1955).

5. See Jaakko Hintikka, "*Cogito, Ergo Sum*: Inference or Performance?" in *Descartes: A Collection of Critical Essays*, ed. W. Doney (Garden City, N.Y.: Doubleday Anchor, 1967), pp. 108–39.

6. W. Norris Clarke, S.J., "Interpersonal Dialogue: Key to Realism," in *Person and Community: A Philosophical Exploration*, ed. Robert Roth, S.J. (New York: Fordham University Press, 1975), pp. 141–53.

7. See C. S. Peirce, "Questions Concerning Certain Faculties Claimed for Man," in *Collected Papers of Charles Sanders Peirce* I–VI, edd. Charles Hartshorne and Paul Weiss (Cambridge: The Belknap Press of Harvard University Press, 1931–1935), 5.213–63.

8. See David Hume, *A Treatise of Human Nature*, Bk. III, Pt. I, Sect. I (Garden City, N.Y.: Doubleday Dolphin, 1961), pp. 412–29.

9. For a survey of opinion of ethical and value judgments, see M. Warnock, *Ethics Since 1900*, 2nd ed. (Oxford: Oxford University Press, 1966).

10. See, e.g., Kurt Baier, *The Moral Point of View: A Rational Basis for Ethics* (Ithaca: Cornell University Press, 1958).

11. For a readable account and critique of relativism, see C. N. Gifford, *When in Rome: An Introduction to Relativism and Knowledge* (Albany: State University of New York Press, 1983).

12. For an informative yet brief article on Nietzsche, see Richard Schacht's "Nietzsche," in *The Encyclopedia of Religion*, 10 (1987), 438-41. For a more extended study one might look at F. Copleston, *Friedrich Nietzsche, Philosopher of Culture* (London: Burns, Oates, and Washbourne, 1942), or Copleston's presentation in *A History of Philosophy* VII (Westminister, Md: Newman, 1963). For this presentation of "Postmodernism" I am indebted to Norris Clarke, S.J.; see Appendix IV.

13. For a brief but clear presentation of Structuralism, see E. Leach's "Structuralism," in *The Encyclopedia of Religion*, 14 (1987), 54–64. This includes a good bibliography.

14. For an overview of some of the major figures and excepts from their works, see *Philosophy: End or Transformation?* edd. K. Barnes and T. McCarthy (Cambridge: The MIT Press, 1987). Note the fine bibliographies. See also Michael H. McCarthy, *The Crisis of Philosophy* (Albany: State University of New York Press, 1990) for a remarkable historical overview of the events leading up to the present-day attempt (by Rorty, for example) to end traditional philosophy altogether. McCarthy does not agree with this approach, even though he admits much of the criticism of "traditional" (Enlightenment?) philosophy is justified. He adopts Bernard Lonergan's approach to "Cognitive Integration."

Study Questions

1. List some of the things which motivated philosophers to inquire into the nature and extent of human knowing. Can you think of any more besides those in the text?
2. What sort of puzzles drove some ancient Greek philosophers to become skeptics?
3. What precisely does the term "skepticism" mean and from what Greek word does it come?
4. Name some of the ancient skeptics.
5. What is meant by absolute or universal skepticism?
6. In general, how would one go about showing that absolute skepticism is untenable?
7. Show that absolute skepticism is internally incoherent and so defeats itself.
8. How did Descartes attempt to defeat absolute skepticism?
9. What is it precisely that makes the *Cogito* indubitable?
10. Which of the early Fathers of the Christian Church refuted skepticism by a move very similar to the one used by Descartes? How did his argument go?
11. Why was Descartes not satisfied with certitude found in mathematical truth as an answer to the skeptics?
12. Once skepticism is shown to be untenable, what important conclusion follows?
13. What is meant by the "problem of the bridge"?
14. What precisely are we trying to show in this section on subjectivism?
15. Explain why the alleged "inside/outside" problem cannot even be stated without having answered it?
16. What does solipsism mean? Would it make any sense for anyone to defend that position?
17. To what sort of evidence would one appeal to show that we do know an external world? Could you spell it out in some detail?
18. Is there any experimental evidence to support the claim that we do not know the self as such except in terms of knowing the non-self? Explain.
19. Sum up the main conclusions of this chapter so far.
20. Show that these conclusions imply the notions of evidence, truth, and certitude.
21. Discuss the fact/value dichotomy.
22. How does this imply value-skepticism?
23. How do some positivist/empiricist theories of knowledge imply

skepticism of fact?

24. How have some social scientists and some educators hoped to use the fact/value dichotomy?

25. Can one deny that fact and value are separated without denying that they are distinct? Suppose one denied their distinction, could this also lead to skepticism?

26. In general, what is the position called "relativism" and why is it so attractive to some?

27. What is the difference between relativity and relativism? How is relativism fatally flawed?

28. Sum up the important conclusions of this chapter.

2

Structure of Knowing

KNOWING IS A CONSCIOUS ACT. There are other conscious acts besides: feeling, sensing, believing, doubting, thinking, willing, deliberating, etc. All conscious acts have a common structure. Conscious acts of knowing (cognitional acts) have, besides this common structure, an architecture all their own. In this chapter we will consider both the structure of consciousness in general and the structure of knowing in particular.

CONSCIOUSNESS IN GENERAL

By consciousness in general we mean awareness of our mental acts. It is usual to distinguish between those acts and their content. Thus, the act of sensing red is distinct from the red sensed. Furthermore, our attention can be focused on either the content or the act. In the first case, we have direct consciousness—where the object or content holds center stage. In the second case, we have *reflex* consciousness—where awareness of being aware of the object or content is primary. Notice that in direct consciousness one is concomitantly aware of being aware but does not attend explicitly to that fact. At any moment, of course, one could so attend, and this would be an act of reflex consciousness.

Out of the foregoing considerations comes the basic structure of all conscious acts.[1] They all are bipolar. They always involve a subject positing the conscious act and an object which the act intends or is about. Hence, within consciousness itself—better, constituting consciousness itself—are a subjective and an objective pole or component. This is the basic, general structure of all conscious acts.

Before we proceed further, a warning and a caution are in order. To talk about the objective pole of consciousness as the content of the subject's act can be seriously misleading. In fact, it has misled philosophers into disastrous mistakes in their analyses of consciousness. To speak of the objects of conscious acts as contents suggests that consciousness is a container and the objects of consciousness are the contained.² This leads to the expression "in consciousness," as if those objects were oranges in a crate or eggs in a box. If we add to this the common-sense idea that consciousness is "within" the conscious subject, then the question of how one ever gets "outside" consciousness and "beyond" the subject not only is posed but is impossible to answer. This, of course, is a version of the "problem of the bridge" considered in the previous chapter. If the evidence adduced there for the reality of a non-ego is convincing and solid, then there is all the more reason for avoiding any expression that might suggest that consciousness is to be thought of on the model of a box. In place of the container model, which makes consciousness closed off from the non-ego, let us substitute a relational model, which presents consciousness as essentially open to the non-ego. Consciousness on this model is essentially consciousness of something or other—where the "something or other" may be in any given case an object distinct from and/or external to the conscious subject. Such an "open" model of consciousness involves "intentionality"; that is, it understands consciousness as intending, going out to, its objects, whatever they be in any particular case: external physical objects, other states of consciousness, ideas, cabbages, or kings.

Perhaps the foregoing remarks will become clearer if we consider an historical example. John Locke was a British Empiricist who held that all items of which we are conscious come to us ultimately from the senses. Furthermore, Locke believed that there is a world "out there," independent of the conscious subject. He also believed that we could know that world. His intentions, therefore, were realist and objectivist. Yet he declared that what we know as a result of sense experience (that of which we are conscious through sense experience) are our ideas. He did not say that we are conscious of things—physical objects—through ideas, but rather that those ideas themselves are the immediate objects of consciousness and of knowledge. But ideas are items *in* our heads; they are items in consciousness, and so he had to raise the question as to how we can know that our "ideas" represent things truly, faithfully, veridically. In a word, he had the "problem of the bridge." How can one get outside of consciousness to compare the ideas of things with the things themselves? Locke literally boxed himself inside that container of ideas, consciousness. If we choose an open model of consciousness, we will avoid this sort of puzzle.

Still, the bipolar structure of consciousness does not of itself say anything at all about the status of the objects of consciousness. It does not determine that any of them belongs to the non-ego; it simply insists that a distinction must be made between any conscious act and the object of that act. In the case of the subject's being aware of himself as conscious subject, this distinction would still hold, even though subject and object are identical. The bipolarity of consciousness taken together with an open model of consciousness leaves as a real possibility one's being conscious of objects which belong to the realm of the non-ego. This possibility is confirmed as an actuality, not merely by common-sense conviction, but by the sort of evidence produced in the previous chapter.

In this connection consider the general impossibility of coherently supposing, as the children's round goes, that "life is but a dream." If understood literally, and not merely as a piece of poetic license or rhetorical hyperbole, such a claim is self-defeating, for the same reason that "I know nothing whatsoever" or "I doubt everything" is inconsistent. Suppose life were but a dream; then such a suggestion could not occur to anyone. To put it another way: if life were but a dream, then the dream would be reality. The only way one could entertain the possibility of life's being but a dream would be by knowing the difference between dreams and reality. Hence, all such literary devices are to be understood as forceful ways of making quite another point: namely, that in some particular cases it is extremely difficult to decide whether an experience is purely subjective—a dream—or objective—an experience of a reality independent of the subject. Such particular cases are to be settled, if settled at all, on empirical evidence. They do not come under a general philosophical thesis.

Any conscious act, then, is intrinsically structured by a relation between subject and object. Without such a relation, consciousness is impossible. Hence, the recognition of the role of the subject in such acts does not necessarily imply subjectivism. Nonetheless, what the objectivity of any conscious act, and in particular of any cognitional act, means is a complex question. While we will not attempt to analyze it in this chapter, still it may not be amiss to indicate some of the questions involved.

A claim to objectivity for any cognitional act may mean any or all of the following:

1. that the object grasped in such an act is *external* to the knowing subject. This implies that such an object is spatially distinct from the subject, that is, occupies a different part of space and to that extent at least is independent of the subject.

2. that the object grasped in such an act is simply *distinct* from the subject and independent from the subject, in the sense that the subject's knowing it or thinking it does not constitute the object's reality. This does not entail that the object be spatial.

3. that what is asserted is not merely biased or an idiosyncratic opinion.

Finally, being conscious is not merely a matter of taking a look at one's mental acts. Consciousness is not some sort of inward look. It is easy to fall into this way of considering the matter if one thinks of knowing as taking a look at or contemplating something, and if one thinks of consciousness as a kind of knowing. The point is that consciousness is not necessarily knowing, even though knowing is necessarily conscious. Furthermore, it will be shown that knowing is not merely a matter of taking a look, even if taking a look is usually involved in knowing.

Consciousness, then, is merely an awareness immanent in our mental acts. It consists in awareness of some content or object and an awareness of that awareness. Not all conscious acts are deliberate; nor are all conscious acts cognitional. Let us now consider the general structure of cognitional acts.

Knowing in General

Knowing involves several conscious acts of different kinds which are related in an incremental and cumulative way to produce the formal act of knowing in the sense of justified true belief. Let us call them *cognitional acts*.[3] These acts constitute the following incremental and cumulative stages in the knowing process: (1) *presentation* through sensing, perceiving, imagining; (2) *understanding* through conceptualizing patterns and structures immanent in those presentations; (3) *judgment* through affirming or denying that proposed patterns and structures for understanding the presentations are correct. This third act is the stage of reasonableness in which by reflection one grounds thought in sufficient evidence (by reflection one grasps the virtually unconditioned).

These stages are incremental in that each successive conscious act presupposes the previous. Thus, there is no understanding unless something is presented to consciousness to be understood. There is no intelligent inquiry unless there are questions for intelligence to answer, that is, questions about what kind of thing we are presented with, and there are no such questions unless something is presented to intelligence. Likewise, there is no reasonable affirmation unless intelligence has proposed answers to those questions raised by what has been presented to consciousness. Nor is the human subject satisfied with proposals concerning the way in which such presentations might be understood. It is not enough to propose hypotheses as to what the immanent intelligibility of the sensuous presentations *might* be. The ultimate question to be answered for reasonable affirmation is "Is it so?"

It follows that these stages are cumulative. There can be no reasonable affirmation unless there has been intelligent inquiry into what immanent intelligibility a sensuous presentation may have or is likely to have. Again, there is no intelligent understanding unless there are data available to the conscious subject which both raise intelligent questions and suggest intelligent answers. The data or sensuous presentation is a given and as such is open neither to question nor to doubt. It must be prior to both.

Finally, these stages form an invariant structure that remains constant across the various ways in which human beings know. Human knowledge may be theoretical or practical; it may be about what is actual or what is possible; it may be about the necessary or about the contingent. Hence, we have various disciplines and their particular methods: mathematics, physics, philosophy. We also have common-sense judgments as to what is to be done here and now or about how to make this or that. No matter what the difference between these various ways of knowing, however, in every case there is presentation, understanding, and judgment.

Because this structure is invariant, it is essentially incapable of revision. The very act of revising that structure would involve its use. The only reason for revision would be some question about its correctness. Is this the structure or not? But the answer to that would entail a review of the evidence, and such a review would include the understanding of what the structure is. This in turn would require a review of the data of which the structure is the immanent intelligibility.

Knowing, therefore, is a conscious act of a subject in which the immanent intelligibility of some object presented to it for understanding is intelligently understood and reasonably affirmed. To know is to answer these questions raised by sensuous presentation: What sort of thing is this? and Is my answer correct? The first type of question is called a question for intelligence; the second, a question for reflection.

Origin of "Ideas"

The term "idea" has been used very loosely by philosophers. Here we will continue in that tradition and designate "idea" to mean any "content" or object of any cognitional act, whether of perceiving, understanding, or judging. The question arises whence these ideas come. The Rationalists (Descartes and Leibniz, for example) and the Empiricists (Locke, Berkeley, and Hume, for example) were divided on the issue. In general, the Rationalists held that "ideas" are innate, that is, inborn, while the Empiricists held that they come to us through experience, that is, through the senses. In general, the Rationalists distrusted, and hence tended to diminish or dismiss, the senses in human knowing. Descartes does consider three possible sources of our ideas: (1) experience (adventitious ideas), (2) mental construction (factitious ideas), and (3) the mind itself (innate ideas).[4] But in the end all veridical ideas (clear and distinct ideas) are innate. The senses are at best the *occasion* for an innate idea's rising to consciousness, but they are never the *cause*. On the other hand, the Empiricists generally distrusted pure reason as a source of knowledge, and hence tended to limit its role to grasping logical or analytic truths (that is, truths that are so by the very meaning of the terms used to express them). All genuine knowledge of the world comes from sense experience as its cause. The human mind is like a blank tablet (*tabula rasa*) on which ideas are written by the senses as the physical world is encountered. Roughly speaking, the Rationalist position traces its beginning to Plato; and the Empiricist, to Aristotle.

The truth of the matter is somewhere in the middle. Sense and reason each contribute to human knowing, and the real issue is to discover just what. Leibniz himself suggested as much when he replied to his Empiricist critics, who cited in favor of their own position Aristotle's maxim "Nothing is in the intellect which was not first in the senses," that the maxim needed to be amended to read "Nothing is in the intellect which was not first in the senses, except the intellect itself."[5] By this he meant that the human mind itself has a structure according to which it actively knows—even if it were a blank slate with regard to content (what experience writes on it), it is not blank with regard to its capacity to receive that content and to grasp it in the act of knowing. This capacity at least is innate.

To determine more precisely what role the senses and the intellect, respectively, play in human knowing is the task of this course. For the moment, however, it will be argued that with regard to *what* we know the Empiricists are more nearly right. There are no innate contents of knowledge. All come to us through sense experience. The evidence in support of the senses as the source of human knowledge is experiential. That "knowledge maketh a bloody entrance" is perhaps all too familiar to us. In any case, it seems that learning is connected with sense experience. No matter how bright our ideas or how ingenious our theories, we are not satisfied until they are put to the test of experience. No matter how abstract our ideas, we communicate them through sensory symbols and we entertain concomitantly with those ideas sensory images (e.g., perhaps diagrams, mathematical formulae, etc.). Our ideas of purely spiritual beings are always developed through negation of sensory properties and by analogy with items in experience. If one is born without the use of one or more senses, one never has an idea of the quality attained by that sense (thus, a person born blind has no idea of color). In short, the Empiricists are right when they insist that every idea, no matter how abstract, spiritual, or lofty, can be traced back to some set of sensory impressions.

The senses, then, are our gateway to the world. They are the source of all our information about whatever is other than ourselves. Even what we know about ourselves is rooted in knowledge of the other which comes to us through the senses. There is much more to human knowing than sensation, but without sensation there is no *human* knowing. The senses present to us what is to be understood and affirmed. Understanding goes beyond sensing to grasp pattern, structure, form; affirming goes beyond understanding to being and to a grasp of the *de facto* absolute. Still, human understanding has no determinate content except what the senses present or imply; human affirmation posits no determinate existent except from what the senses provide or demand.

The rest of this book will consider in turn the role played by sensation, conceptualization, and judgment in human knowing. At the end some brief attention will be paid to other sources of knowledge such as memory, inference, and human testimony. These, it will turn out, are special cases of knowing in general, and so understanding them will suppose understanding of knowing's general structure. In a word, we are trying to understand human understanding, to know what it is to know. If we can make this explicit and consciously appropriate it into our conscious lives, we will, as Bernard Lonergan puts it, "not only . . . understand the broad outline of all that there is to be understood, but . . . possess a fixed base, an invariant pattern, opening upon all further development of understanding."[6]

Let us turn to a consideration of the role of sensation in knowing—the stage of presentation.

Notes

1. See, e.g., F. Van Steenberghen, *Epistemology* (New York: Wagner, 1949), pp. 88–98.

2. See K. T. Gallagher, *The Philosophy of Knowledge* (New York: Fordham University Press, 1982), pp. 44–67.

3. Lonergan, *Insight*, chap. 1.

4. Descartes, *Meditations* III, in *Philosophical Works of Descartes* I, pp. 157–71.

5. G. W. Leibniz, *New Essays Concerning Human Understanding* 2.1.2., trans. A. G. Langley, 3rd ed., 2 vols. (La Salle, Ill.: Open Court, 1949), pp. 00–00.

6. Lonergan, *Insight*, p. xxviii.

Study Questions

1. Define: consciousness in general, direct consciousness, reflex consciousness.

2. Explain what it means to say that the structure of consciousness is bipolar.

3. Contrast the "closed" and the "open" models of consciousness. Which is to be preferred and why?

4. How did Locke regard consciousness and to what problem did it lead?

5. Does the bipolar structure of consciousness of itself guarantee that the objects of consciousness are distinct from the ego or the self? What more is needed?

6. Show that to suppose that everything is a dream or an illusion or an hallucination is incoherent.

7. Cognitional acts are one kind of conscious acts. What might a claim to objectivity for cognitional acts mean?

8. Are conscious acts merely a matter of taking an inward look? What, then, are they?

9. Of what cognitional acts is knowing constituted?

10. Show that these stages are incremental and cumulative.

11. Show that these stages are invariant and thus incapable of essential revision.

12. Compare the Rationalist and Empiricist accounts of the origin of "ideas."

13. How did Leibniz amend the Aristotelian maxim "Nothing is in the intellect . . ."? Any truth to the emendation?

14. What evidence supports the Empiricists' rejection of innate ideas?

15. What is the task of the rest of this book?

3

The Role of Sensation

BY SENSATION we will mean the chain of effects on the knowing subject which are traceable immediately to the operation of the senses. Sensations are as varied as the senses themselves. Whether sensation is a cognitional act has been challenged in recent times.[1] Some philosophers prefer to restrict "sensation" to the causal chain of physical, physiological, and psychological processes that are required for each of the senses to operate properly. We are not conscious of these processes, and in that sense they are not formally cognitional. On the other hand, we might call them virtually cognitional in that they are necessary for the process of knowing, which, admittedly, remains inchoate until understanding and affirmation supervene.

Those philosophers who prefer to look on sensation as causal rather than cognitional frequently use the term "perception" to designate the threshold of cognition. As they use the term, it implies consciousness of what is perceived and includes *conceptualization*. According to this view, that of which we are aware through the senses in perception is always a *this-such*, where "this" indicates the concrete particular, while the "such" already classifies it (that is, conceptualizes it). When we become conscious of some red thing, we are conscious of "this red," which supposes the formal cognitional act of judging "this is red." In turn, from such an awareness we abstract the concept "red" or the pure form "redness."

There is a very important point to this use of the term "perception": namely, that we never have pure sensory experience. It is *always* joined with intelligence—the drive to understand and to know. Human cognitive experience is sensitive-intellective. The contribution of each, senses and intellect, to this unified lived experience is isolated and identified by analysis and abstraction. Our lived experience of "this red" can be analyzed into two distinct and irreducible components: a concrete particular here and now (this) and the kind of thing it is (red). Nonetheless, in our study we will use the term "perception" in another sense: namely, the sensory awareness of a totality prior to explicit awareness of it as a totality and prior to explicit awareness of its component qualities. As we shall see, perception in this sense is the work of an internal sense called the central sense. It is not yet formally and consciously conceptualized and thus properly belongs to that aspect of human cognition which we are calling sensation, even though a conceptual element has been at work from the beginning of the lived perceptual experience.

There are, then, three aspects of perceptual experience to be distinguished:

(1) the *actual lived perceptual experience* of the physical object and its properties: this lived experience is sensitive *and* intellective because it involves judgment; it is formally cognitive and properly a knowing;

(2) *perception* as the stage in perceptual experience contributed by the central sense and accounting for the unity in a single object of the various sense qualities transmitted by the sense receptors; and

(3) *sensation* as the initial stage of causal transmission of sensory information through the various sense organs; we are not conscious of this.

THE SENSES

Everyone is familiar with the five "external" senses: sight, hearing, taste, smell, and touch. They are generally called "external" because of the common-sense conviction that through them we are in contact with an external world. These senses are distinct from one another and frequently work in conjunction with one another. It is evident that each of the five senses has a specialized "object" that it delivers: color, sound, etc. For our purposes, however, it seems better to classify the senses in a different way. Instead of speaking about the "external" senses, we will follow James E. Royce in *Man and His Nature*[2] and speak of the *special* senses. They are special because each has its own receptor organ and each has a special material quality that it alone delivers to consciousness. These include the five "external" senses plus several others which, though not external in the sense of delivering to consciousness qualities of the external world, are special in the sense defined.

Royce defines a special sense as a power by which we experience the quality of a material object stimulating a receptor organ. The special senses are:
- Vision, Hearing, Taste, Smell,
- Cutaneous Senses (warm, cold, smooth, hard, etc.), Kinesthetic Sense (movement of bodily parts),
- Vestibular Sense (bodily equilibrium),
- Organic Senses (ache, pressure, nausea, thirst, etc.).

Besides the senses which deliver to consciousness a particular material quality and which have a special receptor, there are other sensory operations that require internal senses. Again with Royce we define internal sense as the power of representing concrete objects in a material way from sensible qualities experienced through the special senses.[3] These internal senses have no special external organ but seem to be the function of areas of the cerebral cortex.

Although there is some dispute among philosophers whether the internal senses are distinct from one another, four such senses are usually enumerated:
- Central (or Synthetic) Sense
- Imagination
- Memory
- Estimative Power.

The central sense is the power by which we perceive, distinguish, and combine sensations into a total awareness of a present object. Thus, sensory objects are presented to us concretely as wholes (as physical objects) made up of several sense qualities coming from different special senses: e.g., this red, hard, hot thing. It is the central sense as defined here which accounts for sensory *perception*, that is, for the total sensory awareness of a material object present to the sense organs. Recent gestalt psychology experimentally confirms the function of the central sense.

Imagination is the power to represent in a sensory way objects that are not present to the receptor organs. It may merely reproduce previous perceptions or combine them into new images. Memory is the power to represent in a sensory way objects of past experience precisely as past. Whether imagination and memory are adequately distinct internal senses is a matter of dispute, because both reproduce images of absent objects. Finally, the estimative power is the power by which we recognize, prior to learning and without understanding, suitable behavior regarding a sensed object. This is what accounts for "instinctive" behavior.

A word should be said about the notion of a sensible quality or a "sensible," as it is called. Consider the experience of "seeing red." This is an actual lived experience which is both an act and a content. By reflection one can come to the idea of "red as seen," and this yields what common sense takes to be a quality of the "object" of sensation. Finally, we can form the notion of red which can or could be sensed under certain conditions. This is what is meant by a sens*ible*—something in the object which grounds the experience of seeing red.

Sensibles are usually classified as "proper" or as "common" depending upon whether they are correlated uniquely with one sense receptor or not. Thus color, sound, smell, taste, etc., are called proper sensibles. They are properties of the object sensed uniquely correlated to the eye, ear, nose, palate, etc. Other sensibles are common because they can be grasped by several (perhaps by all) the sense receptors. They are figure, size (extension), motion, rest, and number.

The list of senses is perhaps longer than one had expected. This is but a first indication that understanding sensory experience is a very complicated matter. We find it much easier to have such experience than either to describe it or to explain it. In order more deeply to appreciate the complexity of our sensory apparatus and to understand more clearly what marvels the various senses are, let us consider one special sense in some detail.

Vision: An Example of Complex Structure

The human eye has been the most comprehensively studied sensory organ of man. Enormous progress has been made in understanding how it works, but much remains mysterious about human visual experience. Just how complex human vision is may perhaps be better appreciated if we review briefly the physiology of the eye.[4]

In some respects the eye can be likened to a camera in that it is a mechanism to produce images on a light-sensitive surface. In the case of the eye, that surface is not photographic film but a field of millions of visual receptors called the retina.

The outer surface of the eye is made up of tough, protective tissue called the *sclera* which at the front becomes the clear outer covering called the *cornea*. Light enters the eye through the cornea, whose tissues are arranged in such a way as to hinder the light's passage minimally. The cornea is the eye's *major lens*. The light then passes through the *aqueous humor*, a watery substance behind the cornea, and then through the *pupil*, a hole formed by a ring of muscles called the *iris* whose outer layer is pigmented, accounting for eye color. These muscles control the size of the pupil (the hole through which light passes) and so determine how much light passes through to the *lens* behind the iris. The lens is composed of layers of tissue (like an onion). It is elastic, enabling one to alter its shape slightly (rounder or flatter), thus focusing the image on the retina. These changes of shape are controlled by the *ciliary muscles* attached to the lens by ligaments called *zonule fibers*. Behind the lens is the *vitreous humor*, a jelly-like substance which helps the eye keep its shape and which acts as a shock absorber. Next, the light passes through the retina to the light-sensitive receptors at the back of the retina.

The *retina* is a complex structure. Unlike the cornea and the lens, the retina is derived from the same embryological tissue as the brain and so can be considered to be part of the brain. The layer of cells at the back of the retina contains two types of light receptors, *rods* and *cones*. Each eye contains about 6 million cones and about 125 million rods. At the center of the retina is the *fovea*, a region virtually devoid of all receptors—a "blind" spot right in the middle of each eye! Around the fovea the cones are most densely concentrated, whereas the rods are mostly concentrated at some distance from the fovea and then drop off in number toward the periphery.

The cones are the receptors that are sensitive to color, while the rods are sensitive only to shades of light and dark. In fact, the various cones are color-specific; that is, certain cones are sensitive to certain colors. Thus red-green color blindness is due to the malfunction or non-function of the cones specific to those colors. Again, the cones are concentrated around the fovea at the center of the retina, and this accounts for the fact that in day vision we look directly at an object in order best to see it. On the other hand, the rods, which play a major role in night vision, are toward the periphery of the retina; hence, to see an object in very little light, one looks at a slight angle from the object. Once light is received by the eye's rods and cones it is changed into neural energy by a series of complex synaptic connections and sent on to the occipital lobe (rear base) of the brain.

The eye's anatomy, complex as it is, is only a tiny part of the story. There is the anatomy of the rear lobes of the brain to which the receptors send their neural signals. In order for light energy to be changed into neural energy, there is the role played chemically by a substance called rhodopsin. Rhodopsin is a complex chemical containing retinene (related to vitamin A), and opsin, a complex protein molecule. To understand vision, therefore, one must know chemistry as well as anatomy and biology. And, then, that would still be only part of the story. Vision requires light. But light behaves according to laws of physics. Light comes in packets of energy called photons, and photons have properties of particles and of waves (itself a mysterious phenomenon). Not only must one know the laws of electromagnetic phenomena, but one also has to take into account the physical laws by which light is governed in traveling through whatever the medium might be between the light source and the eye. When one has mastered all this—biology, chemistry, and physics—one still has not considered the psychological laws that govern perception in general (e.g., association, adaptation, etc.) and vision in particular.

The point of this digression is to impress upon the reader the enormous complexity of our sensory system. It is like an extraordinarily sophisticated communications network. Signals of various sorts (light waves, sound waves, chemical interactions, pressure) are sent from some source through a variety of media (air, liquids, solids). These signals carry coded messages specific to the proper receptor. Those signals are processed by those receptors and are sent to the brain for decoding. The decoding results in a message: the particular sensory experience. This model of a communications network is admittedly overly simple, but it is a useful first approximation of what is taking place. Every sensory experience has a physical, physiological, and psychological aspect. It cannot be understood unless all these factors are taken into account. Not all these factors are thoroughly understood by science and so, at best, our understanding of one of the most common human experiences is fragmentary. It is one thing to have sensory experience and quite another to understand it.

Describing and Explaining

In like manner it is one thing to describe sensory experience and quite another to explain it.[5] Since description and explanation are often confused, let us try to distinguish them more accurately and more adequately. A first step in this clarification is to notice that the objects of our sensory experience can be considered in two ways: (1) insofar as they are related to us, and (2) insofar as they are related to one another. The first considers those objects precisely *as experienced*, that is, precisely as they present themselves to our sensory consciousness. Two consequences follow: (1) those objects are present to consciousness under whatever conditions, limitations, etc., our sensory apparatus impose on them, and (2) because of that, those objects can be imagined (imaged). The second considers the objects of sensory experience *in themselves*, independently of the way in which we experience them. Two consequences follow: (1) those objects are considered, not precisely under the conditions imposed by our senses, but as transcending them, and (2) hence, the relations of objects to one another need be neither directly perceived nor directly imaginable (only *understood*).

When we describe a sensory experience, we are taking the object described *as experienced*; that is, we are concerned with the object as related to us. Explanation does not necessarily suppose that relation and in most cases in fact does not. Hence, what explains sensory experience need not be experienced. Such explanations, then, usually are not, and frequently cannot be, part of a description of what is experienced. In those cases we are not conscious of the explanatory entities' presence in experience, even though those entities are real. Explanatory entities are the relations of things to one another which are inferred, not directly known, and which are indirectly verified.

There is at least one notable exception to what has just been said. It has to do with explanations of the data of consciousness where in some cases description and explanation merge because the distinction between things as related to us and things as related to one another does not apply.

The first step, then, in coming to understand the role of the senses in human knowing is the attempt to describe that experience. This step would include a description of what is sensed (the data of sense) and a description of the act of sensing (the data of consciousness). A typical account might go something like this: I now see the word processor on which I am typing. It is gray and black, hard to the touch, and emits a peculiar clicking sound each time I strike a key. My awareness of the word processor is vivid, forceful, and lively. I have no real doubt about this experience. My constant mistakes in typing, despite my best efforts, together with the difficulty in finding the apt phrases to write, keep my attention riveted to the display screen.

Such might be a descriptive account of a sensory experience. Notice that this description already uses abstract language and abstract concepts. The predicates are general terms and so already go beyond this particular experience and hence already testify to something more than particular sensory stimuli at work. In a word, description is an act of intelligence—an act of understanding sensory presentations as related to me.

But description is only the beginning of understanding. A further step would be explanation, which is required when questions arise about what has been described. I may wonder *why* the word processor appears gray to me. I may wonder whether it appears gray to anyone else or to everyone else. In effect, I want to know something more than the fact that it appears gray. I want a reason for the fact. I want to know in what grayness consists; what conditions must be fulfilled for one to see an object as gray. In a word, I want to know about the object itself, independently of how it appears to me. I am really asking about the physics, chemistry, biology, and psychology of chromatic vision. Once answers to these sorts of questions are proposed, I am still not satisfied because I want to know whether those answers are correct, that is, whether I have the truth of the matter.

I can merely experience sensory experience; that is, I can merely have consciously a sensory presentation. I may, however, begin to ask questions about that experience and so seek to understand it. The occasion of such reflective thought is frequently some unusual situation which thwarts expectation, e.g., an optical illusion, an hallucination, or generally any discrepancy between appearance and reality. Finally, I want to judge my understanding of sensory experience and thus come to *know* what it is. It is only then that I am satisfied—when there are no more relevant questions about it. Will I in fact ever reach this point of knowledge? Perhaps not, but I come to know that such is the dynamism of intelligence.

Mediation and Inference

In contemporary English the word "mediation" means the act of mediating especially between parties in conflict. More generally, "mediate" means to interpose between two parties or things. It comes from the Latin adjective *medius* meaning "in the middle" or when it is used as a noun (*medium*) "what is in the middle." In philosophy, mediation means what brings together two things. It is a "go-between." The opposite of "mediate" is "immediate," and this properly means "without a go-between." Among philosophers, the question has arisen as to whether or not there is an immediate human knowledge. Strictly speaking, this would mean human knowledge of something without any "go-between," that is, without anything "in-between" the knowing subject and the object known. We will see that those who say that there is such human knowledge have a point but that the point is badly made.

Scholastic philosophers were concerned with whether and how human knowledge is mediated. They made a distinction which we will find useful.[6] What is in-between or goes-between the knower and the known may be any one of the following *media* depending on the kind of cognitional act under consideration:

1. *medium quod*: something which is *itself known* and in knowing *it* something else is known. The usual example of this sort of medium is the premisses of a syllogism. Knowledge of them leads to knowledge of the conclusion. Another might be the words on a printed page, or a traffic light.

2. *medium quo*: something of which one is not conscious but *by which* one knows something else. An example might be the lenses of one's eye-glasses.

3. *medium in quo*: something of which one is not directly conscious in which one knows something else. An example might be a mirror since one sees the image reflected in it without necessarily being aware of the mirror itself (except by a reflective act).

What is of special interest for us is that of the three sorts of media defined above we are directly conscious of only one of them. The other two are really operative without our being aware of them.

Consider inference. In general, inference is the movement of the mind from what is known to what was up till then unknown, that is, a movement from premisses to conclusion. Inferences are of three kinds: deduction, induction, and abduction.[7] Deduction may be characterized as any inferential process in which if the premisses are true the conclusion *must* be true. The conclusion is said to be *necessary* relative to the premisses. Neither abduction nor induction yields necessary conclusions. Their conclusions are at best probable. Abduction is that form of inference by which we conclude to an hypothesis such that, if the hypothesis were true, the premisses from which that hypothesis was inferred would be true as a matter of course. Induction is that form of inference which tests an hypothesis by drawing a consequence as a prediction and then testing for it in experience.

These distinct forms of inference may be illustrated in the following way:

Deduction

RULE: All the beans in that bag are black.
CASE: These beans were drawn from that bag.
RESULT: Therefore, these beans are black.

Induction
CASE: These beans were drawn from that bag.
RESULT: These beans are black.
RULE: Therefore (probably) all the beans in that bag are black.

Abduction
RULE: All the beans in that bag are black.
RESULT: These beans are black.
CASE: Therefore (probably), these beans were drawn from that bag.

Finally, note that inferences are drawn under conscious control. The rules for the validity of deductive arguments and the norms for warranted hypotheses or for correct inductions do not establish how we *must* reason but only how we *ought* to reason. Hence, inference in the proper sense is under conscious control (or at least could be so with a little attention). Strictly speaking, then, there are no unconscious inferences, that is, inferences over which we can have no control. Some philosophers, however, speak as if there were (Charles Peirce, for example).[8] It seems to me that what they probably meant is that certain unconscious processes of perception or of concept formation have a structure *like* an inference. Thus, for example, Peirce likens perceptual predicates to hypotheses because they unify a manifold of sensory impressions just as an abduction concludes to an hypothesis that unifies a manifold of perceptual facts. Henceforth, therefore, when we speak of inference, we will mean inference in the proper sense, that is, as a conscious act capable of control.

Let us, then, define direct cognitive awareness as not involving an inference. By this we will mean that what is delivered to consciousness in such an act is not the conclusion of an inference. Any cognitive awareness the object of which is the conclusion of an inference let us call an indirect cognitive awareness.

Now, at last, we are in a position to consider the role of the senses in human knowing. Our position can be stated as follows: each of our senses, special or internal, is a *medium quo* through which a physical object (and, of course, its sensible qualities) is made present to our consciousness precisely as *this-such-here-and-now* (that is, in its particularity). Such sensuous presentation is *direct* because the physical object so presented is not (consciously) inferred. At the same time it is multiply *mediated* through a complex causal chain, physical and intentional. Any alteration of or interruption in that chain of mediation will alter or terminate our sensory experience. To say that the senses present us reliably (that is, without illusion, hallucination, etc.) with physical objects "under normal (or standard) conditions" means that the mediating chain of causes is operating properly according to the criteria of empirical scientific generalization. Thus, "This *is* red" is analytically equivalent to "This looks red to me under standard conditions," not because "to be red" means "to look red under standard conditions," but because those conditions are standard in which things that *are* red *look* red. Such a position might be called *Direct Mediate Realism*. It is a realism because it holds that physical objects exist independently of anyone's perceiving them (opposed to the Berkeleian "to be is to be perceived"); it is direct because the presence of physical objects is not inferred (opposed to various forms of Indirect Realism such as Lockean Representationalism or Empiricist Phenomenalism); and it is mediate because in its *explanation* of sense presentation it admits a sequence of causes, physical and intentional (opposed to various forms of Immediate Realism such as Naïve Realism).

The twin keys that unlock a clearer understanding of our sensory experience are (1) the distinction between describing and explaining, and (2) the distinction between the *media* of which we are conscious and those of which we are not. The first distinction accounts for the difference between our common-sense account of sensory experience and our scientific understanding of it. Wilfrid Sellars makes this point in terms of what he calls the "manifest image" and the "scientific image" of man, or what Bernard Lonergan characterizes as two domains of discourse, the one using "experiential conjugates" (predicates) to describe experience, the other using "explanatory conjugates" (predicates) to explain it.[9]

On our account of sensation in human knowing, the only correct *description* of sensory experience is in terms of physical objects and their sense qualities. It is of these that we are conscious in such experience and not of the processes, physical, physiological, or psychological, which may *explain* such experience. In perception we are *not* conscious of our "ideas" of physical objects or their sense qualities. We simply do not consciously infer, construct, or otherwise assemble the objects presented to us in a spatio-temporal framework. We simply are not directly aware of "sense contents," "sense data," "surfaces," or any other "idea" from which we then indirectly arrive at physical objects and their qualities. If indeed there are such items, they are explanatory entities posited to account for certain aspects of our conscious experience (perhaps, for example, to explain after-images or memory, etc.). Nor does it help to say that what I directly experience in sensory perception is *merely* appearance ("The apple *appears* to be red to me" rather than "The apple is red") since appearance-terms are parasitical upon physical object language. Hence, it is simply an incorrect *description* of perceptual experience to say that what I experience are my "ideas" (sense contents, etc.). What I experience are physical objects and their sense qualities perhaps *through* or by means of my "ideas." But once I seek to understand how it is that sensory experience presents to me directly (non-inferentially) physical objects and their sense qualities, I move into the realm of explanatory discourse and I posit whatever entities are required to account for such experience (e.g., electrons, photons, nerve endings, synapses, "ideas," "*species impressae*"—none of which is an object of direct perceptual consciousness). All these *explanatory* items are inferred. All these items and the laws that govern their working mediate what directly appears to me in perception, so that if they deviate from their "standard" or "normal" operation, my conscious experience will be appropriately altered (e.g., if the object I see as being red in daylight I now see as purple in blue light, the medium has changed according to physical laws, which, once understood, explain the phenomenon of the object's looking purple while "being" red). Once I understand the laws of refraction of light, that the stick "looks" bent in water is no longer a scandal calling into question the reliability of the senses. On the contrary, the stick's appearing bent is precisely what I expect under the "abnormal" or "non-standard" conditions. If the stick did not appear bent, I would be puzzled, since, in that case, the laws of physics would have failed.

Hence, that which is presented to me (of which I am conscious) directly in perception is a physical object with its qualities. What *explains* such presentation are the multiple media, physical, physiological, psychological, of which I am not directly conscious (therefore each of these is a *medium quo*) but which must be operating for me to receive, process, and decode the sensory signal. Its message is the presence to consciousness of a physical object (under standard conditions).

In the next chapter we will consider in some detail a few of the more influential opinions about the role of perception in human knowing found in the history of philosophy. The point will be to see whether our distinctions will help us to understand how philosophers have been led to say some extraordinary things about experience.

Notes

1. See, e.g., Wilfrid Sellars, "Being and Being Known," in *Science, Perception and Reality*, pp. 41–59.

2. J. E. Royce, *Man and His Nature* (New York: McGraw-Hill, 1961), chap. 4, "The Special Senses," pp. 58–69.

3. Ibid., chap. 5, "The Internal Senses," pp. 70–87.

4. See P. Groves and K. Schlesinger, *Introduction to Biological Psychology* (Dubuque: Brown, 1979), pp. 215–60.

5. The development of this distinction comes from Lonergan, *Insight*, passim, especially chaps. 8, 9, 10, 16, and 17.

6. See B. Wuellner, s.j., "Medium of Knowledge," in *Dictionary of Scholastic Philosophy* (Milwaukee: Bruce, 1956) pp. 74–75.

7. This discussion of inference follows Charles S. Peirce's analysis. See his *Collected Papers*, 2.619–631.

8. See, e.g., ibid., 5.182ff.

9. Sellars, "Philosophy and the Scientific Image of Man," in *Science, Perception and Reality*, pp. 1-40; Lonergan, *Insight*, pp. 79–82.

Study Questions

1. What do we mean by "sensation," and in what sense are those acts cognitional?

2. How are we using the term "perception"? Do all philosophers use the term in this way? Explain.

3. Define "special sense." Make a list of those special senses which we have.

4. Define "internal sense." List the internal senses that we have and explain their function.

5. What is the difference between proper and common sensibles? Give examples of each.

6. Show that the senses are complex structures. Use an example.

7. Can one understand and explain the working of the senses by common sense? How then? What is the point of this whole section?

8. In what two fundamental ways can the objects presented to us in sensory experience be considered? Explain.

9. What consequences follow from considering the objects of sensory experience as related to us?

10. What consequences follow from considering the objects of sensory experience as related to one another?

11. Distinguish description from explanation.

12. What is meant by "data of sense" and "data of consciousness"?

13. How does the distinction between description and explanation apply to our analysis of the role of the senses in human knowing?

14. What is the difference between experiencing sense experience, understanding sense experience, and knowing sense experience? What are we seeking?

15. What does the Latin word *"medium"* mean?

16. Define *"medium quod"* and give an example. Are we conscious of this medium?

17. Define *"medium quo"* and give an example. Are we conscious of this medium?

18. Define *"medium in quo"* and give an example. Are we conscious of this medium?

19. What is inference?

20. What are the three kinds of inference?

21. How does deductive inference differ from the other two?

22. What does it mean to say that the rules of inference tell us how we *ought* to reason and not how we must reason?

23. What consequences follow from that fact?

24. In what sense, if any, might one speak of unconscious inference?

25. Distinguish "direct" from "indirect" cognitive awareness.

26. State the essentials of the position we defend concerning sensory experience.

27. What are the twin keys to understanding this position? Explain.

4

Other Positions on Sensation

LET US TAKE A CRITICAL LOOK at some alternate accounts of the role played by sensation in human knowing. Our review will be *critical*, in that we will try to show what is right and what is wrong with the various positions considered. These positions will be laid out on logical rather than purely historical grounds. They will, therefore, represent *logically possible* positions concerning sensation rather than what has actually been held historically by philosophers. Of course, in some cases (perhaps in many cases) the logical position considered has in fact been advocated by some thinker.

REALISM AND IDEALISM

The terms "realism" and "idealism" have had many meanings in Western philosophy. In general, as the etymology of the words suggests, "realism" attempts to locate what is non-fictitious, what does not depend on mind (finite mind, at least) for its existence. "Idealism," on the other hand, attempts to locate the paradigmatic, what is beyond the changing and the contingent, and, therefore, frequently identifies this immutable with mind—with "ideas" or "ideals." Sometimes "realism" becomes synonymous with "material," because the non-fictitious, the mind-independent, is identified with the non-ego, and the non-ego in turn is identified with matter. In this sense of "realism," "idealism" comes to mean the "immaterial" or the "spiritual," in the sense of what is mind-dependent. For some (e.g., certain materialists), the "ideal" then becomes the "fictitious," because mind (the ego) is reducible to a special manifestation of matter (an "epiphenomenon" of matter).

Because these terms have had so many different meanings (the above paragraph gives only a few by way of illustration), let us define how we will use them. We will use the terms in two different, but related, contexts: (1) epistemological, that is, as they relate to theories of *knowing*, and (2) ontological, as they relate to theories of *being*. In the epistemological context we will use "realism" to denote any theory that holds that we know, directly or indirectly, physical objects and their sense qualities as constituting a world independent of any finite mind (the world of the non-ego). Any other theory of knowledge which makes physical objects and their sense qualities dependent upon their being perceived by some finite mind we will call "idealism." In the ontological context we will use "realism" to denote any theory of being which admits that there are at least some non-fictitious entities which are not mind or spirit, which, in short, are material (whether "material" be construed as substance or as function). Any theory of being according to which the real consists exclusively of mind or spirit we will call "idealistic."

Several things should be noted in connection with these definitions:

1. It is logically possible to be an epistemological realist and an ontological idealist. I could hold that I know, directly or indirectly, physical objects and their sense qualities as constituting a world independent in existence of my knowing, thinking, or willing—hence, a world of the non-ego—and yet hold that the ultimate reality of these physical objects consists in their being "ideas" or "thoughts" and hence ultimately not material substances at all. In this case my ontology would consider matter to be a special (degenerate) case of mind (e.g., the American Pragmatist Charles Peirce) or it would consider the very notion of matter being a substance self-contradictory (e.g., the British Empiricist George Berkeley).

2. Most likely there never has been a philosopher who was an epistemological idealist as we defined it. Berkeley is sometimes presented this way, but I think that such an interpretation misses the point he wanted to make. It was not so much epistemological as ontological; that is, Berkeley was concerned to show that there is no such thing as matter or material substance as defined by the Newtonians. According to Berkeley, Newton's matter was an abstraction and hence a fiction. Furthermore, epistemological idealism entails absolute skepticism and/or absolute subjectivism (solipsism), both of which have already been shown to be literally

absurd.

3. Finally, it is logically possible to be a realist (epistemological as well as ontological) in conviction and in intention, and at the same time hold a theory that implicitly denies realism (at least epistemological realism). Such, I think, is the case with John Locke, as we shall see.

Before leaving our brief discussion of Realism and Idealism, let me point out that "Realism" is also used in the context of another philosophical problem to be discussed in a later chapter: namely, the problem of the "universals." In that context the opposite of Realism is not Idealism but Nominalism. We will consider this at some length when we deal with the role of concepts in human knowing, but for the moment be sure that you understand the context in which the term "Realism" is being used.

Direct Realisms

The position which we outlined as our own in the previous chapter is a Direct Realism. Here we will consider other versions of Direct Realism in order better to understand how our own differs from them.

"Naïve" Realism

"Naïve" Realism is really not a philosophical position at all. It is nothing more or less than the pre-critical common-sense acceptance of what is (or at least seems to be) directly presented to us through the senses, namely, a world of physical objects which are there and are what they seem to be.[1] These objects exist in themselves, independently of our sensing them, and exactly as they are sensed. The total "objectivity" of sensuous presentation is taken for granted. This, in fact, is the working attitude of lived consciousness and is reflected in just about any ordinary description of what we are conscious of in sensuous experience. What grounds this common-sense conviction is our action in the world—our interaction with it—our lived conscious experience. Here there is no concern about discrepancies between appearance and reality, since such discrepancies are not the usual situation of our conscious interaction with the world; insofar as they occasionally do arise, they are handled empirically and pragmatically. In short, for "Naïve" Realism things are as they appear to be.

This last sentence shows both the strength and the weakness of this position (or attitude). Its strength is that it prepares for and looks to action in the world. It accepts common-sense conviction and the common-sense descriptions of the world as sensuously presented to consciousness as basically correct and reliable. In this, our own position agrees with "Naïve" Realism: namely, that the language of physical objects is basic to any description of sense experience since what the senses present to consciousness under standard conditions are physical objects. The weakness of Naïve Realism is that, since it takes perception to be immediate, it does not attempt to understand or explain the unusual sensuous experiences in which appearance and reality conflict. It thinks of sense perception as immediate, and, hence, has no answer to questions concerning the nature of sensation, perception, or knowledge which arise to the reflective mind in the face of such conflict, real or apparent. Hence, most philosophers have tried to elaborate some sort of Critical Realism.

Critical Formal Realism

A Realism is "critical" if it tries not only accurately to describe sense experience but also to explain it. Hence, our account of sensation is critical, but it differs from other critical accounts of Direct Realism.

One such account is Critical Formal Realism. According to this position (held by many Scholastic philosophers), sense qualities, whether proper or common, are "in" the physical objects to which they are attributed just as we perceive them. They belong formally (that is, just as they are perceived) to physical objects. The sensing subject adds or subtracts nothing from those qualities; it merely registers them as present or not. Thus redness is in the red object that we see just as we see it. The object in itself is red regardless of whether any healthy eye sees it under standard conditions or not.[2]

Thus far, Critical Formal Realism does not seem to differ at all from Naïve Realism. They agree in this at least: that we perceive directly physical objects, and the sense qualities of those objects are given to consciousness precisely as belonging to those physical objects (not as some "idea" of those objects or as a "sense content" of an idea of those objects). But Critical Formal Realism goes further. It does offer an explanation of those cases in which there is (or seems to be) a conflict between how an object appears in sense experience and how it is in itself. In general, it explains such conflict by an appeal to a change in or defect of one or more elements in the causal chain connecting the conscious subject and the object of which he is conscious. Thus, a physical object that *is* red (formally has the property redness) *looks* purple in blue light. Once one takes into account that the light is blue and that the object looks purple, one can infer with certainty (hence *know*) that the object *is* red.

Now, such a position is an advance over Naïve Realism precisely in that it attempts to explain discrepancies between how things appear and how they are. Still, this position is not without its difficulties. First, it *assumes* that for a sense quality to be objective it must *be* in the physical object in identically the way in which it *appears* as a property of the physical object as experienced. In effect, this is to assume that knowing is taking a look. It *assumes* that for something to be known it must be imagined. Hence, if we claim to know the sense qualities of a physical object, they must be formally in the object; otherwise, those sense qualities as in the object could not be imagined. It further implies that the objectivity of knowledge rests principally, if not totally, in its character as empirically "given." All these assumptions are open to challenge and indeed are false. Besides, they tend to render the subject passive in sensation. But it might be that the presentation of physical objects to consciousness is essentially relational, that is, the result of the interaction of subject sensing and object sensed.

Perhaps this criticism can be made clear by considering the following:

I see this red object.

This sentence reports an experience. It reports also the object of the experience precisely as it is experienced, namely, as a physical object that is red.

I see that this object is red.

This sentence does more than report an experience and says more about the object of the experience than a mere report of how I experience it. It claims that, independently of my experience of the red object, there is an object and it is red and anyone in appropriate circumstances can verify that claim. Now, the Critical Formal Realist seems to think that my seeing a red object must have the same status as my seeing that an object is red, and so is led to think that an object experienced as red must be the same as an object that is red independently of experience. In the first case, of course, I can imagine a red object as experienced (if my eyes are normal, etc.), while in the second case I cannot imagine an object as red independently of its being seen. I can understand what such a claim means and even know that the claim is true, but I cannot imagine it. When pressed, I think, even the formal realist would be forced to acknowledge that the second claim means that if someone with healthy eyesight looked attentively at the object in question in ordinary sunlight on a clear day, he would experience the object as red. It seems, then, that the claim that an object *is* red comes down simply to claiming that anyone experiencing that object under certain specifiable conditions would experience it in a certain way. This does not entail that the object *is* red when it is not experienced in the same sense as it *is* red when it *is* experienced.

In a word, this position differs from our own in that it does not seem adequately to distinguish explanation from description. It seems to make explanation another sort of description, since what it posits in the object as explanatory must be what is experienced (and hence imaginable), the sense qualities precisely as experienced. This implies that knowing is taking a look and that objectivity is fundamentally empirical.

Critical Virtual Realism

Many Scholastic philosophers under the influence of Locke, Kant, and the findings of empirical psychology concerning sensation have held this position. This form of Realism is direct, in that it insists that *what* is presented to consciousness through sensation is the physical object and its qualities. It denies that any conscious inference is necessary for us to get "outside" our consciousness to reach the physical object (this would be a form of Indirect

Realism of which Locke is frequently accused). For them, consciousness is not closed but open to the non-ego. Still, it disagrees with the Critical Formal Realists in that the proper sensibles at least are not formally "in" the physical objects to which they are attributed (precisely as experienced) but *virtually*.[3] By this, Critical Formal Realists mean that the physical object has the power to cause in us, under suitable conditions, the experience of the physical object, say, as red, or as sounding C-sharp.

This position seems to be even closer to ours than that of the Critical Formal Realists in that the Virtual Realists seem at least to recognize a difference in kind between description and explanation. But unfortunately this is only the appearance, not the reality. In fact, the Virtual Realists still think that objectivity is principally located in the empirically given and that knowing is ultimately taking a look. This is clear from the fact that they limit their Virtual Realism to the proper sensibles. The common sensibles are formally in the physical objects, and it is they that ground the objectivity of sensuous presentation of physical objects. The common sensibles indirectly ground the objectivity of the proper sensibles.

Locke inspired this kind of move, for, in an attempt to save the objectivity of sensation, he distinguished between primary and secondary sense qualities. These correspond to what the Scholastics call the common and the proper sensibles. According to Locke, the primary sensibles were extension, figure, motion and rest, and solidity (impenetrability). The secondary sensibles were color, sound, taste, smell, and touch. He called the primary sensibles "primary" because one could not conceive (imagine?) a physical body without those qualities, while one might conceive (imagine?) a physical body without this or that "secondary" quality.

Furthermore, Locke thought that the secondary qualities could be accounted for in terms of the primary in the sense that certain configurations and motions of extended matter interacting with the various sense organs would produce the various experiences of color, sound, etc. Hence, for Locke the secondary sensibles were formally (as experienced) in the sensing subject but only virtually in the object sensed. In the object sensed, these virtual secondary qualities were formally various combinations of primary qualities. It is evident, then, that the formal secondary sense qualities were modifications of the sensing subject—"ideas"—and in no way resembled the qualities as found in the object sensed. But Locke thought that the primary qualities too were present to consciousness in "ideas." After all, for anything to be present to consciousness it must be a modification of consciousness and indeed it must be "in" consciousness.[4] But this posed a real problem. How are one's ideas of the primary sensibles (in the mind) related to the primary sensibles themselves (in the things)? Locke's answer was by resemblance. I suppose what he had in mind is that physical objects were extended and so were the bodily organs of sense and so there seemed to be a certain homogeneity that might guarantee objectivity—like to like. Such a solution, of course, cannot stand much scrutiny. While it may seem initially plausible to say that my idea of extension is extended, it becomes more difficult to understand that my idea of triangle is triangular or that my idea of motion is moving. So it becomes difficult to say in what such resemblance could consist.

What is more to our purpose than a criticism of Locke is the fact that Locke (and the Scholastics, like Van Steenberghen) thought it necessary to make this move in the first place.[5] It reveals the assumption that the objective is the empirically given and that knowledge is a form of observing (in this case, observing the resemblance or non-resemblance between ideas and qualities).

Our basic criticism of Critical Virtual Realism is that it does not go far enough. It distinguishes the status of primary (common) and secondary (proper) sensibles. But such a distinction will not hold up upon reflection. Berkeley already remarked that our sensory experience of the primary or common sensibles is dependent upon our experience of the secondary or proper sensibles. We never experience just "extension" without some secondary quality—color, texture, etc. We cannot experience figure or shape without some secondary quality—again, color, texture, etc.—by which we are able to discern the boundaries forming the contours of the figure. If there were a homogeneous plenum of "extension," devoid of all secondary qualities, we could not perceive its figure, whether any part of it were in motion or at rest, whether it had solidity or plurality. But then why should the primary qualities be able to guarantee objectivity when the secondary do not? Furthermore, as experienced, both primary and secondary qualities are taken in relation to us; so if the former are "ideas," so are the latter. If ideas are subjective modifications, then both primary and secondary qualities are subjective (Berkeley's *esse est percipi*); if they are not subjective modifications, then both primary and secondary qualities are equally objective (Critical Formal Realism).

According to us, both primary and secondary sense qualities are aspects of the physical object presented directly to consciousness insofar as that object is related to us. But both are presented to consciousness as belonging to the physical object. If we wish to explain how such presentation takes place and to explain how sometimes physical objects only appear to have qualities that they do not in fact have, then we posit theoretical entities (no less real for being theoretical) such as "ideas" or "sense contents" or whatever *by which* and *through which* we experience what we experience.

To repeat: Critical Virtual Realists try to make primary (common) sensibles account for objectivity, because they think of knowing as a looking at (and hence must have an immediate object of the looking) and because they think of objectivity as empirical "givenness" (rather than as what is intelligently understood and rationally affirmed).

Indirect Realisms

Indirect Realisms hold in one way or another that we perceive physical objects and their sense qualities indirectly, that is, by some kind of inference. They seem to require an *immediate* object of perception, and since that immediate object cannot be a physical object, it must be something else—surfaces or sense contents or appearings of some kind. These positions fail to distinguish immediate and mediate knowing from direct and indirect. They seem to hold that if something is directly present to consciousness (i.e., without inference), it must be immediately present, while if something is mediately present to consciousness (as, on our theory, physical objects are), then it is indirectly present (inferred).

This mistake is due to the failure to recognize that not all media in knowing need be conscious (even though one can come to know that there are media involved in the process of knowing). It seems also to overlook that explanatory entities in order to be real need be neither conscious nor known nor, for that matter, even imaginable.

The principal forms of Indirect Realism are Representationalism and Phenomenalism. Let us consider each.

Representationalism

Locke is the classic Representationalist.[6] We have already mentioned that he was, in intention, a Realist and that he tried to guarantee the objectivity of perception by making the ideas of primary sense qualities (which, of course, are in the mind) resemble those sense qualities themselves (which, of course, are in the things). Furthermore, recall that Locke rejected innate ideas. All human knowledge comes from experience. The mind is a blank tablet upon which ideas (the content of the ideas) are written by sense experience. But Locke also said that all we know are our ideas. Hence, the ideas are *what* we know. Locke thinks of the ideas written on consciousness by experience as representations of physical objects or as copies of those objects. If such a model of perception is taken seriously, several insurmountable problems immediately arise:

1. How could one possibly know that one's ideas are representations or copies of anything? To know that something is a copy of something else requires that the "something else" be known independently of its copy.

2. How could one possibly decide whether the representation or copy was faithful to the original unless one knew the original in some independent fashion?

3. How could one possibly know that the ideas of primary sense qualities resemble the qualities in things unless one knew those qualities independently of the ideas?

In general, once one accepts a model of perception according to which ideas (in the sense of contents, not acts) are "in" consciousness and are representations (copies) of things, one is caught in the ego-centric predicament, that is, one is faced with the problem of how to bridge the gap between ideas "in" the mind and things "outside" the mind. An Indirect Realist may try to solve this "problem of the bridge" along the following lines: I have a common sense conviction that physical objects exist independently of my thinking about them. Further, I am conscious that I have no control over the ideas of those objects in my consciousness. Hence, these ideas must be caused in me by objects that have the qualities represented.

This argument supposes that I already know something about the objects of sense experience even before I know the ideas representing them. It supposes that I know that the principle of causality applies to things themselves (and not just to my ideas of things), and it supposes that effects resemble their causes to some degree. But if I knew either of these things, then I would know directly (non-inferentially) something about the physical objects. Hence, if the causal argument works, it is not necessary; and if the argument is necessary, it cannot work (because it is circular).

Again, behind this sort of move is the presumed need to have the objects of perception immediately present to consciousness (in the case of Locke these objects are "ideas"). But this presumption should be questioned, and ultimately rejected in favor of a view according to which physical objects are directly present to consciousness through the mediation of "ideas." On such a view there is no need to think of "ideas" as representations of anything; they are simply the means by which things are presented to (and, hence, are present to) consciousness.

Phenomenalism

Phenomenalism has taken several forms.[7] We must survey some of the more common versions of this position, but first let us recall what the term itself means. The word comes from the Greek verb *phainein* meaning "to show." In the middle voice (*phainesthai*), the meaning is "to show oneself" and hence "to appear." The English word "phenomenon" comes from the Greek verb's present participle, middle voice, and so means "what is showing itself" or "what is appearing." In some contexts, the English usage takes on the overtone of "the appearance" or "the mere appearance" (as opposed to reality).

In general, Phenomenalism posits as the immediate object of perception some item, not itself a physical object, in terms of which perception of the physical object is to be understood. These items (sense contents, sense data, etc.) are themselves *perceived* and, hence, are what is immediately grasped in conscious sensory experience. In perceiving them, therefore, we perceive physical objects and so they function as *media quae*. Remember that Direct Realism claims that the basic thing of which we are directly aware in perception is the physical object. Direct Realism need not deny either that there are sense contents or that we can know *that* they are. It denies that we are directly aware of them in conscious perceptual experience. Hence, if there are such items, Direct Realism interprets them to be *media quibus*.

Remember that sense contents are introduced by proponents of Phenomenalism to account for the fact that sometimes things appear different from what they are. Thus, an object can appear to be red without being red—it merely looks red.

For Phenomenalism, then, we immediately perceive sense contents and believe in (or infer) physical objects. This position differs from the representationalist view in that, for the phenomenalist, sense contents are not copies or pictures of physical objects. Still, Phenomenalism runs into the same kind of problems as representationalism does in that it cannot justify its belief in, or inference to, physical objects without vicious circularity.

The sense contents of Phenomenalism have been characterized in different ways: (1) as surfaces, (2) as sense data, (3) as "existential appearings." Each version is slightly different, and yet one leads to the next. Let us consider each briefly.

Think of a juicy red apple. One might want to say that it is red at the surface but white on the inside. This thought might lead one to think that what one immediately perceives as red is the apple's surface (the surface facing one and seen in normal light). Now, if surface means "the skin" of the apple, then, of course, the skin is just another physical object and one has not yet said anything to which a Direct Realist would object. But one might further insist that one is not talking about the skin or about any other physical object, but about a surface—a two-dimensional color expanse which, since it has no depth, is not a physical object. "Surface" in this sense is an item introduced as the object of immediate perception. Is this item part of the physical object, or is it an "idea"? Either alternative is possible; that is, neither alternative is self-contradictory. One might hold that "surfaces" are just those parts of physical objects (and so can exist unperceived) which are perceived, while the rest of the physical object (the inside of the apple or the surface of the apple on the far side) is inferred or otherwise believed in. But then, there remains the problem of how a surface which is a constituent part of a physical object can appear other than it is (appear to be purple when it *is* red). One then might appeal to "abnormal" conditions in which the surface is seen, but then the surface might just as well be treated as a physical object: the apple is red at the surface under normal conditions but appears purple at the surface under abnormal conditions. (Notice that the following inference is invalid: the apple is red at the surface; therefore there exists a surface and it is red.)

Because the above interpretation, though consistent, is not more helpful than Direct Realism in explaining how something can appear to be red while not being red, one might want to say that the "surface" is an "idea." Now, the surface is a sense content or a sense datum. Since it is not itself a physical object or a constituent part of a physical object, it cannot exist unperceived, but it can account for a physical object's appearing purple when it is red; namely, one is immediately experiencing a purple sense content. On such a theory, then, to experience the apple as red or as purple or as whatever implies that a red or a purple sense content exists whether or not the apple *is* red or *is* purple. The reason is that to have such an experience is by definition to have such a sense content in consciousness.

It follows that an advocate of this form of Phenomenalism (sense content, sense datum) would argue that the sentence

The apple *is* red

is elliptical (and so, strictly speaking, ill-formed). For the apple to be red means simply that I experience a red sense content when the apple is seen under normal conditions. Similarly, the sentence

The apple *looks* red

means that I experience a red sense quality whether the apple is red or not. Hence, any sentence in the form

$$\text{X looks Phi to S}$$

entails that a Phi sense content exists, although the sentence

$$\text{X is Phi}$$

does not entail that a Phi sense content exists, but only that such a sense content would exist if X were experienced under certain circumstances. Hence, that X is Phi is not directly experienced but inferred.

Yet another form of Phenomenalism avoids talk both of surfaces and of sense contents. It uses the language of appearing. Thus,

> The apple appears red to me
> at some time and in some place.

Such an analysis does not commit one to sense contents even though these are compatible. It leaves the analysis at "appearings," however that is to be further understood.

Such a sentence is probably best construed as a *report* of how I experience the apple, namely, as red. But the sentence

> The apple appears to me *to be* red

is not a report but a hedge upon the claim that the apple is red (perhaps because in the past there were times when the apple appeared red when it was not). Again the sentence

> The apple *only* appears to me to be red

is to *reject* the claim that it is red.

The upshot of our consideration of various forms of appearing-talk is that it is of little use for understanding what it is that we perceive and how it can be that something appears to be what it is not. If the appearing-talk is construed as a report, it is autobiographical and not a claim about what appears. If it is construed as either hedging or denying a claim about what appears, it is parasitical upon physical object talk, since to say that

> The apple appears (or only appears) to be red

means that the apple seems to have a property which some apples in fact do have. Hence, for an apple to seem to be red, some apple or other must *be* red.

These last remarks contain the fundamental criticism of any form of Phenomenalism. Talk of surfaces or of sense contents or of appearings all supposes talk of physical objects. In the end, each of these theoretical items has meaning only by reference to my experience of physical objects, and so that experience cannot be described in those terms (even though my experience of physical objects might be *explained* in terms of some such items since, then, these items are not directly experienced). So "surface" has meaning only by reference to the surfaces of physical objects; sense contents have meaning only insofar as they are how a physical object is perceived under certain spatio-temporal conditions.

Finally, at the root of the Phenomenalist move is the assumption shared with all the other opinions about the role of sensation surveyed: namely, that knowing is taking a look (hence, if we are to know the explanation of perception, the explanatory entity must be perceived) and that objectivity is the empirically given.

Much more could and perhaps should be said about the role of sensation in human knowing. For the moment, however, we will be content if the reader is convinced:

(1) that perceptual experience is enormously complex;

(2) that describing a perceptual experience is not the same as explaining it;

(3) that explanatory entities need not be entities of which we are conscious in order for them to be real; and

(4) that of which we are directly conscious in perceptual experience are physical objects and their properties.

The next chapter will begin an examination of another element of human knowing which is already operating in perceptual experience and which is distinct from and irreducible to sensation (or perception). That element is conceptualization.

Notes

1. See Gallagher, *Philosophy of Knowledge*, pp. 68-70 for a brief discussion of "Naïve" Realism.

2. See ibid., pp. 113–19.

3. See ibid., pp. 108–12.

4. Locke, *An Essay Concerning Human Understanding*, chap. 8; see Gallagher, *Philosophy of Knowledge*, pp. 70–83.

5. Van Steenberghen, *Epistemology*, pp. 204–37.

6. Locke, *An Essay Concerning Human Understanding*, Bk. IV, chap. 1. Here Locke says that *what* we know are our ideas, thus compromising his Realism by posing the insoluble "problem of the bridge." He should have said that an idea is that *by which* we know things.

7. This critique of phenomenalism is greatly dependent upon Sellars, "Phenomenalism," and "Empiricism and the Philosophy of Mind," in *Science, Perception and Reality*.

Study Questions

1. Characterize in a general way "realism" and "idealism."
2. How will "realism" and "idealism" be used in this book?
3. How does the naïve realist look on perceptual experience?
4. What are the strengths and weaknesses of Naïve Realism? How does it relate to our position?
5. Explain the position known as Critical Formal Realism.
6. How does Critical Formal Realism relate to Naïve Realism? How is it an advance over Naïve Realism?
7. What are the weaknesses of Critical Formal Realism? What does this position assume about knowledge and objectivity?
8. Through an analysis of the sentences "I see this red object" and "I see that this object is red," give a critique of Critical Formal Realism.
9. How does Critical Formal Realism relate to our position?
10. In what sense is Critical Virtual Realism a Direct Realism? How does it differ from Locke's realism?
11. How does Critical Virtual Realism differ from Critical Formal Realism?
12. Is Critical Virtual Realism closer to our position than Critical Formal Realism? Explain.
13. Relate the common/proper sensibles distinction to the primary/secondary sense qualities distinction.
14. Explain Locke's use of the primary/secondary sense quality distinction.
15. What assumptions about knowledge and reality are behind Locke's use of that distinction?
16. How would you criticize Critical Virtual Realism?
17. What is our position concerning the primary/secondary sensible distinction?
18. In general, what does Indirect Realism hold about perception?
19. Explain Lockean Representationalism. What is its most fundamen-

tal mistake, and what model of consciousness does it suppose?

20. What difficulties does Representationalism face?

21. Why will an appeal to causality not overcome these difficulties?

22. In general, what does Phenomenalism in its various forms hold? What problem is it trying to solve?

23. List three ways in which Phenomenalism has characterized sense contents? Explain briefly.

24. Give Phenomenalism's account of perception using "surface" as the sense content.

25. Show that the "surface" version gives way quickly to a "sense datum" version.

26. Give Phenomenalism's account of perception using "sense datum" as the sense content.

27. Give Phenomenalism's account of perception using "appearing" as the sense content.

28. Show that the fundamental criticism of every form of Phenomenalism is that physical-object language is more fundamental than sense-content language.

29. What does Phenomenalism erroneously assume about knowledge and objectivity?

30. Sum up the main points of our discussion of perception.

5

The Role of Conceptualization

WHEN WE TREATED THE ROLE OF THE SENSES in human knowing, we remarked that our cognitive experience is always sensitive *and* intellective. We always experience through sensation a *this-such*. The basic unit of perceptual experience is the perceptual judgment ("this is a such"), and, consequently, more is involved than just sensing—there is also thinking or conceptualization. While the senses deliver directly to consciousness a physical object with its qualities, the *recognition* that a physical object is a physical object and that its qualities are of various *kinds* (this-here-and-now is a Phi) requires *concepts*.

But what are concepts? Are they some sort of entity, not itself a particular, which is nonetheless real? Are they merely linguistic entities that are shorthand expressions for several individuals? Or are concepts merely elaborated sense images, themselves concrete singulars, which "stand for" many individuals?[1]

Do concepts have any referent in the "real," that is, in the non-mental, world? If not, how and why do they play such an important role in perceptual experience? If so, what is that referent? In other words, are there really natural kinds of things, or are "kinds" merely convenient mental classifications? Are things really related to one another according to law or principle, or are laws and principles merely mental constructs?

Finally, how are concepts formed? Where do they come from? Are we born with them? Do we learn them? Do we derive them in one way or another from sensory experience?

SOME TECHNICAL TERMS

Before considering the classical problem of the universals, let us define some technical terms. A concept is an abstract and general (hence, mental) representation of something. A concept is a *medium* in the knowing process, that is, it mediates between the subject knowing something and what it is that he knows. It is, however, a *medium in quo.* (unlike sensing, which is a *medium quo*) in that while it presents directly to consciousness physical objects precisely as some *kind* of thing, the concept itself can be made the object of conscious attention by an act of reflection. Hence, it is that *in which* (not by which) one knows something. (Note: the implication of this distinction is that the concept has an intentional or epistemic role in knowing and not merely a role as physical cause.)[2]

A concept may be considered *subjectively* or *objectively*. As *subjective*, a concept is the *act* of conceiving or classifying; as *objective*, a concept is the *content* of that act, that is, what the concept means.

Universal concepts are either direct or reflex. A *direct universal concept* is that which can be predicated of many individuals univocally (in exactly the same sense) and distributively (taken one at a time). An example of a direct universal concept would be "human." It can be predicated in the same sense of John and of Peter and of Mary, etc. A *reflex universal concept* is one that names a class and so cannot be predicated of anything. An example would be "humanity." Neither Peter nor John nor Mary can be said to be humanity, although each can be said to belong to the class so named.

Concepts have both a comprehension and an extension. A concept's *comprehension* is its meaning—the notes that define it. Thus, the notes "rational animal" constitute the comprehension of the concept "man." A concept's *extension* is the collection of individuals of which the comprehension can be predicated, that is, the collection of those individuals that exemplify or instantiate the meaning. Thus, the reflex universal "humanity" (or "rational animality") refers explicitly to the concept's extension, namely, to the fact that the direct universal "human" can be predicated of many individuals. In any given use of a concept, one can ask whether one is referring to every individual within its extension or to only some of them.

From the preceding paragraph it should be clear that direct universals intend only the concept's comprehension and prescind or abstract from its extension. It says only *what kind* of thing something is and does not mention or imply whether or how many other individuals there may be of the same kind. Hence, direct universals can be predicated. Reflex universals, however, cannot be so predicated because they explicitly intend the concept's extension and so name an entire class of things.

Finally, concepts can be either *first intention* or *second intention*. A concept is first intention if the individuals to which it applies are not themselves concepts. Thus, "man" is a first intention concept, because the individuals, John and Mary and Peter, etc., to which it applies are not concepts but physical things. A concept is second intention if the individuals to which it applies are themselves concepts. Thus, the concept "concept" is second intention since no concept is a physical thing. This distinction is analogous to that made by contemporary logicians between *object-language* and *meta-language*. An object-language is the one we use to talk about items in the world, while a meta-language is the one we use to talk about the language we use to talk about the world. Thus, English can be used both as an object-language and as a meta-langsuage. Clearly, we use English to talk about the world, but we also use English to talk about English as a language—grammar, syntax, logic, etc.

THE CLASSIC CONTROVERSY: THE PROBLEM OF THE UNIVERSALS

The problem of the universals exercised some of the best minds of the Middle Ages.[3] Some maintain that the answer to that problem is still, even now, the key issue in philosophy. The problem in the Middle Ages was frequently posed in terms of genus and species (while today we might put it in terms of scientific laws). Genus and species are abstract representations of *kinds* of things. "Animal," for example, is a generic concept, in that it can be further logically determined to, say, "rational animal" where "rational" is the specific difference narrowing the genus to a logical species. Logical species, of course, is also a "kind," but such that it cannot be further essentially determined. Under it are subsumed individual exemplifications or instantiations (e.g., John, Mary, Peter, etc.). More generally, however, the problem might be posed in terms of any of the predicables, that is, classifications of the relations of predicates to subjects (genus, species, specific difference, property, logical accident).

The problem was this. Universal concepts are abstract and general representations. Existing things, however, are concrete and particular. What, then, if anything, do universals represent in the existing things? Is there any "correspondence" between what the universal concept represents abstractly and in general and the concrete particular? What sort of information, if any, do universal concepts deliver about those concrete particulars?

Exaggerated Realism

As you might expect, there were two extreme positions proposed as solutions and several compromises in-between. The extreme positions were *Exaggerated Realism*, on the one hand, and *Nominalism*, on the other. Let us consider each of these viewpoints briefly.

The Exaggerated (or Extreme) Realists took their inspiration from Plato (or at any rate from the Platonic tradition). They held that we do indeed have concepts and that they have ontological counterparts in the real (non-mental), if not the physical, world. These realities to which our concepts correspond (grounding their objectivity) are the Ideas or Forms. These Forms are not in the physical objects; nor are they themselves physical objects. Nor yet are they abstract ideas, since, then, they would be concepts and would exist only in our mind. They are *absolutes*, neither individual things nor abstract ideas, located in a domain beyond or transcending the physical world and, according to Christian Platonists, "in God's mind." These Forms are immutable and eternal. They are the paradigms according to which God creates things. The things which He does create are said to "participate in" those Forms (exemplify them?). St. Thomas Aquinas, following the Persian philosopher Avicenna, called these Forms (Divine Ideas) *universalia ante rem*, that is, "universals before (prior to) the thing (created reality)."

Thus, for example, the abstract concept "man" is grounded in the Form "Man" or "the Man." Similarly, the abstract idea "horse" is grounded in the Form "Horse" or "the Horse." And this goes for all other predicates: red, hot, tall, hard, running, walking, sitting, etc. (Note: Plato himself had trouble with this.)

Such an explanation may have seemed all well and good as an account of the ontological grounding of created things, but for it to have an epistemological value it had to be supplemented by a theory that posited forms also *in* the individual existing things to which our abstract concepts referred. In other words, there also had to be *universalia in re*, that is, "universals in the created thing." Things had to have "natures" or "essences" in terms of which they "participated in" (or perhaps "exemplified") those transcendent, absolute Forms. William of Champeaux (1070-1120), an Extreme Realist, is alleged to have held that the nature or essence of anything—say, of man—is unique and identical in all the individuals of which "man" can be truly predicated. Thus, the individual is merely an accidental modification of a nature or essence. Now, the consequences of such a position are rather difficult to swallow, and Peter Abelard, William's student, was quick to point out the problem (not too diplomatically either!). If William's understanding of *universale in re* is correct, then since Plato is a man and Socrates is a man, and since there is only one unique human nature, Plato is Socrates!

Nominalism

It was difficulties like that which prompted other medieval philosophers to give another, equally extreme, solution to the problem of universals. Nominalists simply denied that there are any concepts that are distinct from linguistic expressions. As it is sometimes put, in words attributed to a certain Roscelinus (1050-ca.1120), concepts are *"mere flatus vocis"* ("merely the sound of a word"). In general, Nominalism maintained that in nature the individual thing alone exists. There is no such thing as a *"universale in re,"* at least as understood by the Extreme Realists. While this denial of a unique nature of which individuals were merely accidental modifications was a step in the right direction, it was weak in not exploring the ways in which language (in which concepts are expressed) might be related to the things (their properties and relations) which concepts signify. Nominalism was correct in recognizing that abstract and general properties, precisely as abstract and general, do not exist outside the mind—they are not *things* (*res*). To say that they are just words, however, is hardly enlightening.

This weakness called for correction. One move was to distinguish between the word in the material sense (the letters which make it up, the sounds which articulate it in speech) from the word's meaning. Among grammarians writing in Latin a word with a meaning was called a *nomen*, while a word in the sense of a collection of letters or of sounds was a *vox*. The point of the distinction was to identify the concept with the meaning. Hence, a concept is not a "mere word" in the material sense but a significant word, a word with a meaning.

Once this distinction was made, it was possible to hold that concepts are, indeed, not merely linguistic entities. To what, if anything, they corresponded in things, however, was still an open question. *Conceptualists* argued that concepts corresponded to nothing at all in things, since real existent things are through and through individual, concrete, and particular. But if there is nothing in things to which concepts correspond, then concepts do not have their origin in things. In a word, we do not "get" concepts from things; rather we "put" concepts onto things. Concepts exist only in the mind, and they can come only from the mind (perhaps constructed by the mind, perhaps innate to the mind). Again, for these philosophers, there are no natures or essences *in* things; essences or natures are at best ways in which we think of things; essences are only "nominal," not real.

Moderate Realism

There was still another group of medieval thinkers who were satisfied neither with Extreme Realism nor with Nominalism (and its conceptualist modification). For want of a better term, this group has become known as the Moderate Realists. Abelard (twelfth century) is usually counted as an early precursor of this movement and Thomas Aquinas (thirteenth century) as its most sophisticated proponent. The key to Moderate Realism's solution to the problem of the universals is to be found in Aristotle. In this regard, Aquinas had a decided advantage over Abelard, since he had available to him works of Aristotle (translated into Latin) which Abelard did not. The principal Aristotelian elements incorporated into Moderate Realism are the theory of the individuation of form by prime matter and the theory of abstraction.

The Moderate Realists accepted the following as true and so

as defining the problem to be solved:

1. The only things that exist are particulars;

2. Universals as universal, that is, as predicable of many (reflex universals), exist *only* in the mind;

3. What universals signify (their comprehension) are immediately grounded in things, but ultimately grounded in the Divine Ideas; hence, there are in some sense universals in things and universals prior to things;

4. All our concepts come from experience; hence, there are no innate ideas.

Clearly, the Moderate Realists agree with the Nominalists in points 1 and 2. They agree partly with the Extreme Realists in point 3, but must find a way of explaining how the universal is *in* the thing which avoids making Plato and Socrates one and the same human being. Finally, in point 4 they must find a way of accounting for the origin of concepts which avoids both innatism (say, Platonic reminiscence) and sensism (concepts are nothing but words that stand for several sense images). Aristotle's metaphysics and psychology provided solutions to the problems posed by points 3 and 4. Let us see how.

Aristotle's metaphysical analysis of an existing physical object (a concrete and individual particular) rested on the distinction between prime matter and substantial form. Substantial form accounted for how several distinct individual substances could be of the same kind. Each had the same substantial form but in each case that form was received by prime matter and individuated. Neither substantial form nor prime matter was a thing; rather, each was a co-principle, and *together* they formed this-thing-of-a-certain-kind. As co-principles (not things or physical parts) of each individual, prime matter and substantial form were *transcendentally* related, that is, the very existence of each principle depended on its being related to the other. Hence, for Aristotle, form was in each individual but as individuated by matter (therefore, not an abstract concept or an absolute Idea in a Platonic heaven).

Now, with this metaphysical distinction within individual particulars, there was logical space for a theory which could claim that indeed individuals (say, Plato and Socrates) were, as concrete existing substances (the composite of matter and form), substantially (not merely accidentally) distinct, and at the same time could claim that the substantial form, considered abstractly, was identical in each and as such grounded the concept whose comprehension was the form in the abstract in the things. This came to be known as the theory of the two *esses*.[4] Form can exist in two ways: (1) physically, insofar as it is individuated by matter forming the composite existing physical object; and (2) mentally, insofar as it is considered by the mind in a total abstraction from matter, the co-principle which individuates Form. The Form is the objective content of the concept (its comprehension), and on this theory it is the same both in the concept and in the thing but with two different modes of existence.

Now, this solution supposed that the mind has the power to consider form apart from matter.[5] Such a power was called abstraction. The formation of a concept was the direct result of the exercise of this power. The Scholastics (e.g., Aquinas) considered this power to be spiritual precisely because it enabled man to prescind from matter and to consider form by itself.

Roughly, abstraction was thought to work something like this. Through the operation of the senses, a perceptual image of a physical object was impressed upon the mind (*species impressa sensibilis*). This impressed species or image was called a phantasm. Man's active or agent intellect discerned in and abstracted from the phantasm the form (its intelligible pattern), and in turn impressed this form on the passive intellect (the intellect's capacity to receive form). This form was called the *species impressa intelligibilis* (the intelligible impressed species). Having received this intelligible form, the passive intellect (now informed with the species and hence now in act) expressed it (after the analogy of expressing a word, in this case, a mental word), and this *species expressa intelligibilis* (expressed species or mental word) was the concept.[6]

The solution just considered is essentially Aquinas' adaptation of Aristotelian principles. So that you will not be misled, note that the solution of Aquinas was not the only one (or indeed the most popular one) in the Middle Ages. Scotus, for example, had a different theory, and his student, Ockham, had yet another.[7] For now, suffice it to say that Scotus, although he used Aristotle, tended to emphasize the Platonic elements in the Scholastic tradition, and that Ockham sympathized with the Nominalist-Conceptualist position. In fact, Ockham is considered to be the originator of modern Nominalism.

Lastly, to fill out our picture of Aquinas' solution, let us see how he used a distinction from Avicenna. We have already introduced the terms *universale ante rem* and *universale in re*. The first referred to the Divine Ideas in God's mind (the Platonic Forms); the second, to the substantial form in things individuated by prime matter. There was a third universal, *universale post rem*, "the universal after the thing." This referred to the concept in the mind, which, since it was abstracted from the thing (via the senses), was *post rem*.

This scheme sums up Aquinas' view nicely and manifests how one medieval thinker looked at man as made in God's image. God creates the things of this world according to the Divine Ideas (*universalia ante rem*) which He has of them. God creates in the strict sense, in that things are as He wills them to be. Man is made in God's image and likeness, precisely in that he too can know the created world and act upon it. Man's knowing and willing, however, do not constitute the natures (substantial forms) of things (*universalia in re*). Man merely discovers what these natures are through perception and intellection. Man's "creative" power is manipulative of things, not constitutive of them. Hence, man abstracts concepts (*universalia post rem*) of the natures God created. Man, the knower and doer, is, as it were, the mirror image and likeness of God the Creator.

This solution seemed to meet the problem of the universals as it was defined by the medieval disputants, and this solution is ingenious. Many philosophers today hold some such theory. Respectable as it is, however, most contemporary philosophers find it unacceptable as it stands.[8] Why, we will consider in the next chapter.

Summary and Conclusions

We began this chapter by stating three questions which must be answered if one is to have an understanding of the role of conceptualization in human knowing:

1. Are there concepts which are neither merely words nor merely confused sense images? (What is the nature of concepts?)

2. Are concepts in any way grounded in the world of physical objects in such a way that they genuinely inform us about that world?

3. How are concepts formed?

We have seen how various medieval thinkers attempted to answer these questions. Of those solutions we have suggested that the best of them is along the lines of Moderate Realism and more particularly that of Thomas Aquinas. It might be useful to retrace the Thomist answers to those questions in a more systematic and argumentative way.

To the first question, then, the Moderate Realist would answer that there are mental representations called concepts which are neither mere words nor sense images. The typical argument cited in support of this claim is that unless there are such concepts predication would be impossible. But if predication were impossible, judgment would be impossible. And if judgment were impossible, knowledge would be impossible. But the consequent is false and therefore so are the chain of antecedents.

Since absolute skepticism has already been shown to be untenable, the only point in the above argument which needs further clarification is the claim that predication is impossible if concepts are merely words or sense images. This claim hangs on an understanding of predication as the identity of the predicate with the subject in any proposition of the form S *is* P. What is meant by "predication by identity" is something like this: (1) when one asserts "John is a man," one is not asserting a relation of part to whole, since neither is being a man part of being John (while some other part of being John is not being man) nor is being John some part of being man since being man is totally exemplified by John; (2) on the other hand, such an assertion is not the material identity of being man and being John, since then one would be asserting either merely that John is John or that John is the only possible man; (3) one is asserting, therefore, that a certain form, being man, is exemplified concretely by John. John *is* a concrete case of being man. The identity of subject and predicate, then, is sometimes said to be *objective*, in the sense that being man and being John are both true of John.

Given this understanding of predication, it is clear that concepts could not be merely words in the material sense (that is, mere *voces*). The assertion that John is a man does not mean that John is the word M-A-N. This suggestion is just so silly that we can be confident that no philosopher ever held it. It might make more sense to say that there are no concepts, that words stand immediately for the things to which they have been associated, say, by ostensive definition (pointing to the things). On this interpretation we would have a theory that makes all meaning to consist in pointing to things. But this surely will not do, since there would be no sufficient reason for assigning the same word to any group of objects unless one recognized that they had something in common, that is, unless one had a concept of their structure or form. Besides, not all meaningful words (*nomina*) refer to items that can be pointed out.

Concepts cannot be simply sense images because no matter how vague the image, no matter how "average" it may be, it is still singular and particular, and no particular can be predicated of another by identity. Thus, if the concept "man" were nothing but a vague image of a man, then I could say that John is something like that image but not that he *is* that image. Furthermore, I could not recognize the similarity without referring both John and the image to a third thing: namely, the concept of the aspect in which they are alike.

Besides, there are concepts which can be understood but which cannot be imagined. Thus, I can understand what a million-sided polygon is, but I cannot form an image of it. A similar thing might be said of the concepts justice, love, democracy, and so on. This is not to deny that some sense image may accompany any such concept, but it is to deny that the concept *is* the image. Moreover, there is reason to think that one's understanding of something and one's ability to image it vary inversely. For example, the more one progresses in science, the more difficult it is to form an image of what one understands.

To the second question (whether concepts are grounded in things) the Moderate Realist would again answer in the affirmative and offer negative and positive reasons to support his view. Negatively, he would argue that unless concepts are grounded in things, we would not have any knowledge of them. The reason is that knowledge is expressed in judgments, judgments are formulated in propositions, and propositions are made up of concepts. But if nothing in things corresponds to our concepts of those things, then propositions cannot say anything about those things and judgments would not assert anything about them.

Positively, the Moderate Realist might argue that we are positively aware that our choice of concepts to characterize what we experience is not arbitrary but determined by the object experienced. Furthermore, it is a fact that a person deprived from birth of one of the special senses (e.g., sight or hearing) cannot form any proper concept of the corresponding sense quality. Thus, a person born blind has no concept of color. This would be difficult to explain if there were no connection between the concept and the object presented to sense experience. Finally, the Moderate Realist might point out that our concepts allow us to operate in and upon the world with great success, and this would be all the more remarkable if those concepts were in no way grounded in that world.

To the third question (how concepts are formed) the Moderate Realist would reply with the theory of abstraction as elaborated above. This needs no further treatment here, except to say that in the opinion of most philosophers after Kant, including some of the most prominent Thomists (Rousselot, Maréchal, Rahner, and Lonergan), this is the most vulnerable part of the Moderate Realist's position. Why and how its weakness might be strengthened is the topic of the next chapter.

NOTES

1. See R. I. Aaron, *The Theory of Universals* (Oxford: Clarendon, 1952), passim, for a clear and comprehensive review of the problem of universals.

2. For one famous interpretation of Thomas Aquinas in the matter of conceptual knowledge, see Jacques Maritain, *The Degrees of Knowledge*, trans. G. B. Phelan (New York: Scribner's, 1959), chap. 3 and Appendix I; for a sense of the variety of opinion within "Thomism," see H. J. John, *The Thomist Spectrum* (New York: Fordham University Press, 1966), passim.

3. Besides Aaron's *Universals*, see F. Copleston, *A History of Philosophy*

II (Westminster, Md.: Newman, 1950); M. De Wulf, *History of Medieval Philosophy*, trans. E. C. Messenger, 2 vols. (London: Longmans, Green, 1926), passim. For some contemporary treatments of the problem from several points of view, see, e.g., N. Wolterstorff, *On Universals: An Essay in Ontology* (Chicago: The University of Chicago Press, 1970); H. Staniland, *Universals* (Garden City, N.Y.: Doubleday Anchor, 1972); P. Butchvarov, *Resemblance and Identity: An Examination of the Problem of Universals* (Bloomington: Indiana University Press, 1966).

4. See, e.g., P. Coffey, *Epistemology* I (New York: Longmans, Green, 1917), pp. 269ff.; Gallagher, *Philosophy of Knowledge*, pp. 153–78.

5. Bernard Lonergan, S.J., *Verbum: Word and Idea in Aquinas*, ed. D. Burrell (Notre Dame: University of Notre Dame Press, 1967), pp. 141–82. Form was called the *species impressa intelligibilis* (the intelligible impressed species).

6. In *perception* we are aware of no image or phantasm but rather of the physical object itself; hence, in perception there is no *species expressa sensibilis*. The *species impressa sensibilis* (sense impression) is enough, since it is a *medium quo*, a cause, not the object, of perception. In memory and imagination, however, we seem to be aware of images or phantasms, and hence there seems to be need of a *species expressa sensibilis* over and above the *species impressa sensibilis* (sense impression) as that in which the absent physical object (or event) is re-presented to consciousness.

7. See, e.g., Copleston's *History of Philosophy*, vol. II for Scotus and vol. III for Ockham.

8. See, e.g., among the Scholastics Lonergan's criticism, in *Insight*, pp. 87–89.

Study Questions

1. What three central questions need to be answered concerning concepts?

2. Define "concept" and discuss the type of *medium* it is in human knowing.

3. Distinguish what was Abelard's criticism of William of Champeaux's position?

4. Define direct and reflex universal. Why cannot a reflex universal be predicated of anything?

5. Distinguish a concept's comprehension from its extension.

6. Define "first intention" and "second intention" concept.

7. How did medieval thinkers understand the "problem of universals"?

8. What was the position called Exaggerated or Extreme Realism?

9. What is meant by *"universale ante rem"*?

10. What is meant by *"universale in re"*?

11. What did William of Champeaux hold concerning *"universale in re"*?

12. What did the Nominalists hold concerning universals?

13. How did Conceptualism try to remedy Nominalism's weakness?

14. Who is considered the most sophisticated medieval proponent of Moderate Realism and what doctrines from what ancient Greek philosopher did he incorporate into his position?

15. List four propositions held to be true by the Moderate Realists which defined for them the problem of the universals.

16. Give Aristotle's analysis of the metaphysical composition of a physical object (his theory of matter and form).

17. According to Aristotle, how are matter and form related? Explain.

18. How did this metaphysical view help Aquinas formulate his solution to the universals?

19. Explain how Aquinas' abstraction works.

20. What use did Aquinas make of Avicenna's distinction between universals before, in, and after the thing?

21. What does a Thomist mean by "predication by identity"? Explain.

22. What arguments would a Thomist who is a Moderate Realist with respect to universals offer to show that concepts are not merely words?

23. How would he argue that concepts are not sense images?

24. What negative argument would a Moderate Realist propose to show that concepts are grounded in things?

25. What positive argument would he offer?

6

Judgment

THUS FAR WE HAVE CONSIDERED the roles of sensation and of conceptualization in human knowing. Each is an *aspect* of the cognitional process, but neither is yet human knowing. Sensation and perception, considered apart from conceptualization, simply provide the materials for knowing. Whether it be the physical object present to consciousness in direct perception or the sensible image (phantasm), representing to consciousness physical objects once directly perceived, these are only potentially understood and potentially known. Conceptualization, considered apart from judgment, simply allows us to *think* the materials provided by sensation and perception. Conceptualization is the beginning of understanding, in that it classifies and relates as a *such-and-such* the *this-here-now* of sensibility tentatively and hypothetically. The question remains whether such classification and relating are *correct*. Such classification and relating need to be verified, that is, it must be shown that the evidence is sufficient to warrant the assertion in each case "It is so." Only then is knowing complete, for only then is any truth-claim made.

JUDGING

Judging is the act of the mind by which a proposition is grasped as virtually unconditioned, that is, as having sufficient evidence for its assertion as true.[1] Many traditional presentations of judgment ascribe to it a dual role.[2] The first is *composition and division*. This refers to the act of formulating a proposition in the form: S is (not) P. The idea, of course, is that understanding unites or divides the subject and the predicate to form an affirmative or a negative proposition. There is nothing intrinsically wrong in making this a function of judgment, provided one realize that the act of judging is still incomplete. It requires that the proposition be affirmed or denied, and this is another and different act.

Hence, the second role of judgment on this traditional presentation is precisely *affirmation or denial* of a proposition. Such affirmation or denial is justified in terms of sufficient evidence. It would be a serious mistake to think that an analysis of how propositions are structured is identical with an analysis of their affirmation or denial.

To make the matter clearer, it might help to relate judgment as affirmation or denial to some other familiar items. Consider the relation of utterances, sentences, and propositions. If you say "The book is red" and I say "The book is red," there are two utterances—two separate speech acts—but only one sentence has been spoken. Again, notice that when I typed the sentence "The book is red" twice in this paragraph, I wrote the *same* sentence twice. There were two writings of it, but only one sentence (there are two *tokens* of a *type*). Now, suppose I say "The book is red" and you say "*Das Buch ist rot*"; now there are two distinct utterances (or writings) *and* two distinct sentences (since German is not English), and yet there is only *one* proposition; that is, what is meant is identically the same. But whether you understand English or German or both, when you hear these sentences and understand their meaning, you may or may not assent to them. You may merely consider them. Only when you assent or dissent to them have you made a judgment in the full sense.[3]

There are two sorts of questions which we put to ourselves when something is presented to us to be understood: What is it? and Is it so? Let us call the first sort a question for intelligence (understanding) and the second a question for reflection. Judgment in the full sense requires an answer to the question for reflection, although it supposes an answer to the question for intelligence. Judgment, then, supposes a personal commitment to the proposition's truth and the assumption of a certain responsibility for affirming or denying it.

The process of knowing is differentiated, cumulative, and incremental. It is differentiated into distinct, and even separable, stages: presentation of something-to-be-understood; understanding of pattern or intelligible form emergent in the presentation; and judgment as to whether such pattern or form is in fact verified in the presentation. This process is cumulative, in that judgment depends upon understanding and understanding depends upon presentation. One may experience presentation without understanding; one may have an understanding without knowing that it is correct, but the reverse is not possible. Finally, this process is incremental, in that each successive stage adds something to the former without which the process would fail to come to a satisfactory outcome. One passes from a to-be-understood to a possibly-the-correct-understanding to the-correct-understanding (the truth of the matter). When one reaches correct understanding by grasping evidence as sufficient (the proposition as virtually unconditioned), one knows, that is, one has justified true belief.

Each single correct judgment is an increment in knowledge and, in the context of inquiry, brings one of the steps to conclusion. Still, various pieces of knowledge and various steps in any inquiry are interrelated. Inquiry takes place within the context of logic and dialectic. Logic looks to the ordering of pieces of knowledge acquired in any stage of an inquiry. It seeks coherence among the elements and asks for the implications of their relations. Dialectic, however, looks to the situation when such organization and coherence break down and some new stage is about to begin. In such a breakdown situation, a conceptual framework has been expanded to its breaking point, and a new one needs to be found. For example, the Aristotelian framework for motion broke down with the experiments of Galileo and Newton; it gave way to a new mechanics which in its turn was developed and expanded by logic until in its turn it had to yield to quantum mechanics. Oddly enough, it is the orderly, coherent, logical development of a framework's implications which, as it goes deeper and deeper, brings the framework to its limits where it breaks down and dialectic takes over to find a higher viewpoint.

Judgments are contextual with respect to time. Present judgments are related to past judgments, which remain with us forming our habitual orientation toward the world. Our habitual orientation influences our attention, our evaluation of insights, our openness to new insights, etc. Present judgments (those made now or in the recent past) are also related, for instance, as conflicting, as compatible, as complementary, etc. Conflicting present judgments, for example, may set off the dialectical attempt at resolution, while compatible and/or complementary present judgments invite logical development into a coherent whole. Finally, present judgments are related to future judgments, in that the present state of our knowledge determines what new questions can arise and so in what ways we can add to our habitual knowledge.

Finally, it is only in the act of judging that the question of truth arises.[4] Neither sense presentations (whether in perception or in memory/imagination) nor concepts are formally true or false. In themselves they are simply whatever they are. It is only when something is asserted as being or not being the case that the question of whether one has gotten it right arises.

Evidence: The Virtually Unconditioned

At this point it would be well for the reader to review what was said in the Introduction concerning the structure of evidence as sufficient. Recall that evidence is sufficient when one has grasped the virtually unconditioned, that is, when one has grasped the conditioned as having its conditions fulfilled.[5] Hence, a judgment is virtually unconditioned: (1) if it is conditioned; (2) if its conditions are known; (3) if the conditions are fulfilled. How these if's are fulfilled we must consider in a general way and then in a few particular cases.

Insight is the grasp of an intelligibility immanent in the data. Insights are vulnerable or invulnerable; that is, either they settle the issue at hand or they do not. The issue at hand is settled just in case there are no more pertinent and relevant questions to be asked about it. The settling of an issue does not exclude the raising of *other*, perhaps connected, issues (and, in fact, usually does raise them), but the issue at hand is resolved. For example, I may be able to settle the issue that during the day my house burned down but still be at a loss to know what caused the fire. Nor is it enough that as a matter of fact I do not think of any further pertinent or relevant questions concerning the issue at hand since this may be due to my ignorance or laziness or inattention. There must *be* no such questions. To be able to recognize such a situation I must have in hand both timidity and boldness, for in the one case I would not judge when I should (He who hesitates is lost!) and in the other I would judge when I should not (Look before you leap!). How this balance of temperament is acquired is not easy to say; nor is it a simple story. It has to do with one's learning, training, experience, and character. In general, it supposes that one is disposed to allow further questions to arise, if there be any. This means an openness to evidence. Bias is the enemy of such openness. It supposes a background of other correct insights in terms of which one can pose the correct question (without which there is no correct answer). Finally, to break this apparently vicious circle, it supposes the process of learning which is self-correcting (clearly in the case of judgments of fact, like "my house burned down") through the shock of experience.

With these admittedly very general observations in mind, let us consider briefly several kinds of judgment with respect to how evidence is grasped as sufficient or not.

JUDGMENT OF FACT

By a judgment of fact I mean a contingently (not necessarily) true judgment about some event or state of affairs in the world. I take it as non-controversial that all events in the world are conditioned, that is, depend for their occurrence on other events. I assume that this is also the case with states of affairs. A correct or true judgment of fact, then, asserts something conditioned as obtaining in the world because its conditions are known and are known to be fulfilled. What we want to consider is *how* such a judgment is made—what cognitional acts are involved.

Lonergan gives the following simple example.[6] A man returns home to find his house in a shambles, smoke in the air, and water on the floor. Cautious by nature, he judges, "Something happened." This is a judgment of fact, however anemic; if it is true, it is so contingently; and the judgment about the event is conditioned. The conditions to be fulfilled are in the notion of change (something happened): namely, that two different sets of data be true of the same subject at different times (continuity and diversity). Those fulfilling conditions are grasped in two sets of data: the present perception of the state of his house and its remembered state at an earlier time. Both sets of data are referred to the same set of things called his house. This is a structure immanent in consciousness and exists prior to any statement about them. If the process is expressed in statements and if those statements are affirmed, they are judgments. But it is the structure immanent in the cognitive process which links the conditioned with the fulfilling conditions.

Perhaps one other example of a concrete judgment of fact will help make the point. Besides the factual judgments based on the data of sense (perceived and/or remembered), there are judgments of fact based on the data of consciousness. One such is, "I am a knower."[7] I am a knower if I posit certain kinds of acts: perceiving, thinking, conjecturing, believing, judging, willing, and so on. Those conditions are known to be fulfilled precisely through my being consciously aware of positing them. It is a contingent matter of fact that I am a knower and not a necessary truth; yet I cannot deny that I am a knower since the act of denial itself shows that the conditions for my being a knower are fulfilled. Hence, the evidence for this judgment of fact is sufficient. This is (or should have been) Descartes' point in appealing to the *Cogito*.

There is, then, at least one correct judgment of fact. But it is in terms of correct judgment of fact that concrete analogies, generalizations, and judgments of common sense are justified. But not all judgments are judgments of fact and not all judgments can be supported by sufficient evidence. In a word, some judgments are by their nature only probable.

Probable Judgments

Probable judgments fall somewhere between the absolute affirmation or denial consequent upon the grasp of sufficient evidence and a simple avowal of ignorance.[8] Probable judgments, however, are not to be confused with judgments of probability. Judgments of probability assign to runs of events a ratio of successful outcomes to total possible outcomes using the calculus of probability and statistical methods (e.g., sampling). Judgments of probability, insofar as they reflect the empirical situation, anticipate that actual runs of events will diverge from an ideal frequency, but only at random. Thus, while it is analytically true that the probability of tossing heads with a fair coin is exactly $1/2$, what such a judgment anticipates about the tossing of this particular coin is that, if it is not weighted and if it is not tossed in a special way designed to favor a particular outcome, then the ratio of heads to heads-and-tails will oscillate at random about the value $1/2$.

Probable judgments, however, arise from the incomplete state of our knowledge about a situation. They are not just guesses, but still the evidence is not sufficient to exclude all further pertinent and relevant questions. They are "educated" guesses. Or, perhaps, the best guess given the available evidence. While such judgments do not attain the virtually unconditioned, they have such attainment as their norm. We might say that probable judgments approach or converge on the virtually unconditioned. This has an air of paradox about it, since it seems that the only way in which we could know that a judgment approaches or converges on the virtually unconditioned is to know the virtually unconditioned. Still, the paradox is not as bad as it may seem, since all inquiry arises from the peculiar state of both knowing and not knowing—of seeking a known unknown. We do not know the answer, but we would recognize it should it come along. This drive to know is at the basis of the self-correcting process of learning and grounds all inductive procedures.

Oddly enough, the conclusions of empirical science cannot be more than probable. Empirical science begins by making significant correlations of data (whether in the form of classical or statistical laws) which define abstract correlatives. But those abstract correlatives have to be referred back to the concrete for verification, and this raises further pertinent and relevant questions. For example, such reference requires measurement, which requires an understanding of the measuring instruments and their physics. In a word, it requires the systematization of an entire field. That systematization itself would not have reached the virtually unconditioned until one knew both that there were no as yet unknown facts which might force a revision of current theory and that there are no known facts which should force revision but which have not been so recognized.

Analytic Judgments

Propositions are said to be analytic if they are true in virtue of their "meaning."[9] What this means is not very clear, and there is no firm agreement among philosophers and logicians about the matter. The problem, of course, is how one understands meaning. One common distinction is between the syntactic and the semantic structure of a sentence expressing a proposition. Then propositions may be analytic in virtue of their logical syntax or in virtue of the definition of terms. An example of the first would be any "logical truth" (that is, a tautology) such as: it is false to say both that p and q is true and that p and q is not true:

$$\sim((p \& q) \& \sim(p \& q)).$$

The reason is that no matter how one assigns the values true and false to p and to q the entire expression always turns out to have the value true. Thus, the following truth table illustrates a typical logical truth:

p	q	(p&q)	~(p&q)	((p&q)&~(p&q))	~((p&q)&~(p&q))
T	T	T	F	F	T
T	F	F	T	F	T
F	T	F	T	F	T
F	F	F	T	F	T

An example of the second would be "A bachelor is an unmarried male," where the predicate defines the subject. These propositions become analytic judgments once they are affirmed.

All other propositions are synthetic; that is, their truth value is determined neither by their logical syntax nor by the semantical meaning of their terms. While it is clear that all analytic propositions are necessarily true, a major philosophical question is whether any synthetic propositions are ever necessarily true. Since Kant, this has been known as the question of the *synthetic a priori*. A word of explanation is perhaps in order.

Kant was trying to answer Hume's challenge to the objective grounding of the causal relation.[10] According to Hume, the essential element in the causal relation was a necessary connection between antecedent and consequent (cause and effect). But Hume claimed that such a connection could be neither observed nor deduced; hence, what accounts for our sense of necessary connection is simply the habit of expecting the consequent given the antecedent because in past experience one has constantly followed the other. This is one of the key ideas in Hume's association of ideas. But if Hume is right, while it may be true that we must think of the world as causally connected, we have no right to say that it *is* causally connected. But for Kant science is precisely the investigation of the world in terms of causal connections and hence Hume's critique undercuts the entire scientific enterprise.

Kant's strategy for answering Hume was to provide logical space for a proposition which was at once synthetic (not a mere logical truth) and necessarily true. Hume thought that there were only two kinds of propositions, logical truths (analytic) and matters of fact (synthetic). Logical truths are necessarily true, but they do not give us any information about the factual world in which we live, since, as necessarily true, they are compatible with any world whatsoever. Matters of fact, on the other hand, do inform us about the world but are never necessarily true. Logical truths are true *a priori*, that is, "before" or independently of experience; all matters of fact, however, are *a posteriori*, that is, "after" or arising from experience.

Now, it was the distinction between analytic and synthetic, on the one hand, and between *a priori* and *a posteriori*, on the other, which gave Kant the key to his answer. He pointed out that while it is true that every analytic proposition is *a priori* and every *a posteriori* proposition is synthetic, it does not follow that every synthetic proposition is *a posteriori*. There is the possibility of a proposition which is synthetic and *a priori*. For Kant a proposition is synthetic if the predicate is not "contained in" the subject. "Gold is yellow" is synthetic since no analysis of the meaning of gold would tell us that it is yellow—it might indeed be white. "7 + 5 = 12" is synthetic in this sense since no analysis of "7 + 5" will yield "12"; it must be referred to the experience of counting. And yet, "7 + 5 = 12" is necessarily true, true in any world (given the axioms of which it is a theorem), and so true *a priori*. For Kant, while all knowledge arises with experience, not all knowledge arises *from* experience, and the synthetic *a priori* is a case in point. The principle of causality is also synthetic *a priori* because while our knowledge of the connection between two objects arises only from experience, the necessity of the causal connection arises only with, not from, experience—the necessary connection comes from the *a priori* categories of the Understanding.

Now, the point of all this is that Kant was right to criticize Hume, regardless of whether one accepts Kant's own account of the synthetic *a priori*. What is needed is some account of how propositions that are necessary can refer to the real world of fact, that is, how they can have "existential import." Rather than follow Kant, I would prefer, following Lonergan, to speak of analytic *principles*.[11] An analytic proposition is also an analytic principle if and only if the terms that constitute part of its meaning are existentially instantiated, that is, if and only if they occur in their defined sense in judgments of fact.

What, then, constitutes sufficient evidence for asserting analytic propositions? The conditioned is the proposed analytic proposition. Its conditions are the meanings or definitions of the terms employed in the proposition. The link between the conditioned and its conditions are the rules of syntax according to which propositions are generated out of those terms. If the terms of those propositions turn out to be existential, that is, if they occur in their defined sense in judgments of fact, then those propositions are also analytic principles (referring to the world).

There are many other sorts of judgments which could and should be examined, for example, mathematical judgments and judgments of common sense. But these will have to be postponed for another occasion. For now we must consider a number of issues which arise from our analysis of the cognitive process: the role of the *a priori*, conceptual frameworks, and theories of truth.

Notes

1. This entire chapter is heavily dependent upon Lonergan's *Insight*, chaps. 9, 10, and 11. I urge the reader to consult this work for more detailed development of the issues raised here.
2. See, e.g., Aquinas, *De veritate* (On Truth) q. I, a. 3.
3. Lonergan, *Insight*, pp. 271–78.
4. See, Aquinas, *De veritate* q. I, a. 3; O'Neill, *Theories of Knowledge*, pp. 63–65.

5. Lonergan, *Insight*, pp. 279–316.
6. Ibid., pp. 281–83.
7. Ibid., pp. 299–304.
8. Ibid., pp. 319–28.
9. Ibid., pp. 304–309.
10. Kant, *Prolegomena to Any Future Metaphysics*, trans. P. G. Lucas (New York: Barnes & Noble, 1953), Preface.
11. Lonergan, *Insight*, pp. 306–309; 315–16.

Study Questions

1. What is understood by the act of judging and how did the tradition characterize it?
2. Relate judgment to utterance, sentence, and proposition.
3. Explain: the cognitive process is differentiated, cumulative, and incremental.
4. Discuss the contextual nature of judgment.
5. Where does the question of truth formally arise? Why only there?
6. What is meant by vulnerable and invulnerable insights?
7. What is meant by judgment of fact?
8. Give an example of a judgment of fact and show how it illustrates the structure operating when we grasp fulfilling conditions.
9. Analyze "I am a knower." Why is this an important example? How is it like Descartes' *Cogito*?
10. What is the difference between probable judgments and judgments of probability?
11. Why are scientific judgments at best probable?
12. What is meant by analytic proposition? Give an example of a logical truth; of a definitional truth.
13. Discuss Kant's understanding of analytic and synthetic; of *a priori* and *a posteriori*.
14. What problem, posed by Hume, was Kant trying to solve with his synthetic *a priori*?
15. Why would Kant say that "7 + 5 = 12" is synthetic *a priori*?
16. What does Lonergan mean by analytic principles? Does it bear any likeness to Kant's synthetic *a priori*?
17. What constitute sufficient evidence for affirming an analytic proposition; an analytic principle?

7

Complementing the Classical View: Abstraction and the *A Priori*

ARISTOTLE BEGINS HIS WORK on *Metaphysics* with the observation "All men by nature desire to know."[1] The Kantian synthesis of philosophy suggests that the philosophical enterprise is the attempt to answer life's three fundamental questions: What can I know? What ought I to do? and What can I hope for?[2] The drive to know, then, is fundamental to being human. From childhood, the human person is characterized by questioning—why? what? what for? In principle, there is no end to our questioning. Even when a particular issue is settled (when we have grasped the virtually unconditioned), other issues arise—endlessly. Of course, one might refuse further questions, but that refusal itself only underscores the drive to know. The only thing that would completely satisfy our desire to find out would be knowledge of everything about everything. But as it is, it seems that while we can know something about everything, we cannot know everything about anything. To put it another way: given anything at all, we can know it to some extent and also know that there is more to be known about it, but we cannot comprehensively know everything about everything. Hence, our achieved knowledge is always limited, and known to be so, while our desire is limitless.

HORIZONS OF INQUIRY

The first move in complementing the classical view is to make explicit this drive to know and its implications.[3] That it was in the classical tradition, we saw with Aristotle and Kant. Aquinas and other Scholastics spoke of grasping the "infinite" in the affirmation of any contingent truth. Here, then, the point only needs some development.

The human person has an open-ended drive to know. In each case where one knows that one's knowledge is limited one is already beyond that limit and oriented toward the known unknown. Intelligence is ordered not merely to this or that kind of thing but to the total horizon of being—to whatever there is. When the Delphic Oracle proclaimed Socrates the wisest of men precisely because Socrates admitted his ignorance, the point was not that Socrates did not know anything, but rather that he realized that he did not know everything and was willing to try to find out.

But fruitful inquiry is never in general; it is always in particular. It is always in terms of some specific set of questions, and those questions are specified by some horizon of inquiry—by some framework or point of view. What horizon of inquiry anyone chooses to pursue at any given time or as a life's work is a function of that person's needs, wants, and desires. The sciences, arts, philosophy, theology, social sciences, technology, crafts—all are horizons of inquiry. Ideally, intelligence would master them all; practically, it must settle for less. Yet through cooperation it can benefit from all.

The fact that an unrestricted desire to know is fundamental to being human invites several important reflections which we can only suggest here. The first has to do with what sort of being humans are. They are not closed within their own space and time, even though they are within some particular space at some particular time. They are in it but not of it. Second, the unrestricted desire to know coupled with known actual limits affecting any given individual invites an openness to learn from others—to a community of inquirers. Lastly, there is room for reflection concerning the relation between theory and practice. If inquiry is guided by needs, wants, and desires, what those needs, wants, and desires are, or are perceived to be, becomes very important. In a word, what is *valued* becomes important. Are those values authentic, genuine? Are they biased, self-defeating? What is the relation between "fact" and "value," between what I do and what I think?

Abstraction

In the chapter on conceptualization we remarked that the Moderate Realist position on universals (at least as proposed by some) has certain weaknesses which must be corrected if it hopes to be taken seriously today. Those weaknesses are (1) a neglect of the *a priori* elements in conceptualization and (2) a neglect of conceptual frameworks and how they function in an understanding of the world. If those weaknesses are not corrected, the theory of abstraction so central to Moderate Realism will be either oversimplified or distorted. One oversimplification is to think of abstraction after the model of Little Jack Horner who, while eating his Christmas pie, merely "stuck in his thumb and pulled out a plum, and said, 'What a good boy am I!'" We just put the thumb of our intellect into the pie of sensible presentation and pull out the universal concept. To put it another way: do we just "read off" universal concepts from our experience? Or do we rather frequently have to work hard to find the apt universal? One distortion of abstraction is to think of it as framing an "impoverished replica" of the physical object rather than as an enriching of sense experience through understanding.

Consider these two basic models of abstraction:[4] (1) impoverished replica of the concrete; (2) enriching anticipation of an intelligibility to be added to the sensible data—an insight into form. Our contention is that model 1 is an incorrect view because: (*a*) it reduces abstract ideas to sense images and thus transfers the property of necessity proper to the abstract over to the concrete and so invites determinism; (*b*) it precludes any coherent account of how scientific laws, both classical and statistical, might be objective. It forces a choice: if one holds that classical laws are objective, then statistical laws are merely a cloak for our ignorance; if statistical laws are objective, then classical laws are merely a convenient shorthand for referring to individual experiences of concrete situations (they are a macroscopic illusion).

The reason for this unhappy dilemma is that if abstraction is merely an impoverished replica of the original full-blooded reality, then, as a replica, whatever properties it has must come from the reality. Hence, if classical laws are the correct abstract representation (replica) of the physical world, then whatever properties those laws have must come from the physical world and so properly belong to that world. But classical laws connect consequents to antecedents *necessarily*, as conclusion to premisses in a deductive argument. Physical events are cases under a general rule, and they can be predicted with absolute certainty and exactitude. The abstract laws after all are merely *replicas* of the physical events. On such a view, one anticipates that reality will always and everywhere with complete exactitude conform to the laws that abstractly represent it. Hence, one would also expect that predicted results and observed results should coincide, "all other things being equal." If they do not, then, either there was "observational error" or else all other things were not equal (that is, some unknown factor was at work).

Again, if abstraction is a mere impoverished replica of reality, then, if statistical laws are the correct abstract representation (replica) of the physical world, then the properties that those laws exhibit come from, and properly belong to, that world. But statistical laws connect consequents to antecedents with degrees of *probability*, as conclusion to premisses in an inductive generalization. Physical events are observed as samples on which to generalize, and future physical events are predicted with *probability* and *approximation*. On such a view, one anticipates that reality will conform "more or less" to our predictions but allowance is made for random deviation. The physical world, then, of which the abstract statistical laws are a replica, is law-like with regularities that hold "for the most part." These regularities admit of random deviation and of the possibility of change.

Notice that these accounts, based on the impoverished replica model of abstraction, are incompatible inasmuch as they ascribe to the concrete events of the physical world properties that belong to abstract generalizations. The concrete events cannot be both necessary and probable, exactly conforming to prediction and "for the most part." Hence, one is forced to choose between classical and statistical laws as the correct replica of the concrete physical world. If one opts for classical laws, then statistical laws can only be a "cloak of our ignorance." We just do not know all the variables involved in formulating the classical law, but in principle we can find them out and when we do the law will predict with absolute precision and exactitude. If, however, one goes with statistical laws, then classical laws turn out to be only a psychological device for summing up aggregates of events (since there are no "forms" in things).

On the second view of abstraction, the following hold true: abstraction (whether that of classical laws or of statistical) (1) involves an enriching anticipation of an intelligibility to be found (by insight) in the sensible data, and hence goes beyond its mere presentation; (2) involves the insight revealing what in the data is significant, relevant, important; (3) involves the formulation of the intelligibility revealed by such insight. Only here does the negative aspect of abstraction appear—the omission of the insignificant, the irrelevant, the negligible. Abstraction merely omits the non-systematic, but does not deny it, and hence leaves open the possibility of an empirical residue (the non-systematic conditions under which the systematic has concrete realization). This second view allows us to distinguish what characterizes the concrete events precisely as concrete, on the one hand, and what characterizes their abstract representation, on the other. In their abstract representation there is no conflict between representing them as exhibiting both classical and statistical aspects. Concretely, individual events are instantiations of types. Their abstract representation allows us to isolate their systematic aspects in classical laws and their non-systematic aspects in statistical laws. The former asks what is the nature of the phenomenon with which we are dealing and the latter asks, granted that we are dealing with a phenomenon of this kind, how often can we expect the concrete cases to conform and to what degree.

Abstraction understood as enriching is closely connected with a proper understanding of the role of the *a priori* in human knowing. Let us consider first Kant's interpretation of it.

THE *A Priori*

Philosophy in the West has never been the same since Kant. His influence has been called the "Kantian turn," and has been praised or condemned but rarely ignored by philosophers since. In general, "the Kantian turn" in philosophizing consists in recognizing in one way or another the active role of the knowing subject in knowing. The subject is no longer considered a purely passive spectator which merely registers in consciousness what objects force on it. In a word, the subject has something to contribute to the object as known—howsoever one understands that contribution.

Still, it would be a mistake to think that no philosopher before Kant had thought of this. Thus, for example, Leibniz, one of Kant's immediate predecessors, remarked, in answer to Locke's attack on innate ideas, that nothing is in the intellect which was not first in the senses *except* the intellect itself. This implies that the intellect has some capacity for understanding what the senses present to consciousness and therefore that the intellect has some structure in terms of which it acts on such presentations. Again, Aquinas, although he was empiricist enough to agree with Aristotle that everything we know comes through the senses, realized that whatever is received by a knower is received according to the capacity of that knower. This implies that the physical object presented in sensation is altered by the subject so as to be received in an intentional (as opposed to a physical) mode of being, for if the subject received the physical object according to its physical mode, the subject would *be* the object whereas the subject only *knows* it.

Kant

Thus, important figures within the Western philosophical tradition before Kant recognized the transforming role of the subject in knowing. None, however, had taken such a radical position as Kant; nor had they attempted to work out in detail what the subject's contribution is. Kant's position was so radical that he himself called it the "Copernican revolution" within philosophy.[5] Just as Copernicus stood astronomy on its head by suggesting that the earth revolves around the sun (against the traditional geocentric view of Ptolemy), so Kant stood philosophy on its head by suggesting that the world as known (the *phenomena*, "things as they appear to us") is determined by the subject imposing on a formless sense manifold the structures, sensible and intellectual, which things appear to have. The object, considered in itself (the thing-in-itself or *noumenon*), is unknowable and merely "raw material," as it were, for sense and intellect to form into the object as known (the *phenomenon*). Kant thought that this novel reversal of the dominant role in knowing from object (determining mind) to subject (determining object as known) was the only way of ensuring truth, where truth is understood as the conformity between object and mind. Since, on Kant's analysis, mind or subject constitutes the object as known (as appearance), object and subject *must* conform to each other. He calls his position "empirical realism" (things are *for us* as they appear to be) and "transcendental idealism" (things as known, *for us*, are constituted as appearances by mind).

It seems fair to say that Kant is trying to spell out just what the structure of "mind" is. He is taking up the suggestion of Leibniz and of Aquinas and giving it a radical twist. All formal or structural elements in the object known (as appearance) come from the structure of mind; all material elements (the sense manifold) are relegated to the noumenal, the unknowable. (Note: Aquinas would have called the sense manifold the *pars materiae* of knowing and the unifying structure of that manifold the *pars speciei*.[6]) These formal elements, coming from the structure of mind alone, are the conditions of possibility of our having any cognitive experience; hence, they themselves neither are experienced as such nor come *from* experience. Kant puts it this way: every element in human knowing arises *with* experience, but not every element in human knowing arises *from* experience (such elements would be *a posteriori*). The formal elements arise *with* experience because, as conditions of the possibility of experience, they are given as fulfilled in experience; but these formal elements do not (and cannot) arise *from* experience precisely because they are its conditions of possibility. Thus, for Kant, all the formal or structural elements in human knowing are *a priori*.

Kant recognized in human knowing two irreducible aspects, one essentially active, the other essentially passive or receptive. The former he called Understanding; the latter, Sense. Sense or the receptive aspect of knowing has its formal, and so *a priori*, character: namely, the forms of Space and of Time. These forms account for our apprehension of physical objects in space and time. In other words, the mind, through its sensible faculty, first organizes the manifold of sensuous presentations under the forms of Space and Time. The result is sensible *intuition* of physical objects as spatio-temporal. This is, according to Kant, an intuition, because the objects so presented are particulars (this-here-and-now). Our grasp of the *a priori* forms of Space and Time is likewise an intuition since those forms themselves are particulars (there is only *one* Space and only *one* Time of which each physical object presented in sensuous intuition is a part). Physical objects do not exemplify Space and Time as John or Mary exemplifies the universal "man"; rather they occupy a part of space and a part of time.

Sensuous intuition provides *content* (spatio-temporal objects) for thought. But those objects are not yet objects of thinking. They become so only when they are subsumed under the formal structures of the active Understanding. These formal structures Kant called *Categories* of the Understanding. When we think about physical objects, we classify them and we put them in various relationships. In a word, we predicate universal concepts of them in various sorts of judgments. According to Kant, these concepts are neither grounded in nor abstracted from physical objects themselves, which have forms independently of, and prior to, our thinking them. To the contrary, the reason why we can think those physical objects as exhibiting such forms (that is, insofar as those objects appear in thought to have them) is that the Understanding has structured sensible intuition with those forms (Categories) *a priori* (independently of and prior to our actually using those concepts in judgment). In other words, the Categories of the Understanding are the conditions of possibility of our making judgments about physical objects (of our thinking them). Just as intuitions, through the *a priori* Forms of Space and Time, provide *content* for thought, so concepts, through the *a priori* Categories of the Understanding, provide *form* for the object thought. As Kant himself says, intuitions without concepts are blind; concepts without intuitions are empty. Together, and only together, do they yield knowledge of physical objects.

Kant thought that the *a priori* nature of the Categories of the Understanding could be "deduced" in two ways: (1) from the various forms of judgment studied by formal logic (the Metaphysical Deduction), and (2) from a consideration of the conditions of possibility of our thinking objects given in intuition (the Transcendental Deduction).[7] The Metaphysical Deduction is concerned with establishing the *list* of categories and with showing their origin in the very nature of human understanding. The Transcendental Deduction is rather a justification (not really a deduction) of the objective validity of human knowledge precisely because the categories must apply to the objects of sensuous intuition (making some judgments universal and necessary).

Hence, in the Metaphysical Deduction, Kant drew upon the formal logic of his day and deduced twelve Categories corresponding to the twelve types of judgments. The following table correlates the logical forms and the Categories:

Table of Judgments	*Table of Categories*
(a) QUANTITY	(a) QUANTITY
1. Universal	1. Unity
2. Particular	2. Plurality
3. Singular	3. Totality
(b) QUALITY	(b) QUALITY
4. Affirmative	4. Reality
5. Negative	5. Negation
6. Infinite	6. Limitation
(c) RELATION	(c) RELATION
7. Categorical	7. Substance
8. Hypothetical	8. Cause
9. Disjunctive	9. Community
(d) MODALITY	(d) MODALITY
10. Problematical	10. Possibility
11. Assertorical	11. Existence
12. Apodictical	12. Necessity

It is important to realize that Categories are not predicates. Hence, they are not direct universal concepts. They are rather the conditions of possibility that there are concepts which can be predicated of things. In this respect Kant's Categories are like Aristotle's Predicaments except that the Predicaments are a classification of predicates (hence are not themselves predicates) rather than conditions of possibility of predicates. (Note: Aristotle listed ten predicaments: substance, quantity, quality, relation, place, time, position, habit, action, and passion.) Kant had the problem of how concepts are formed and applied to objects of thought. He did not have the Aristotelian theory of abstraction to help him. How are the Categories (conditions for thinking) reduced to concepts which can be predicated of things (actual thinking)?

The final item, then, necessary to Kant's account of the *a priori* conditions of possibility of human knowing is the *schematizing* of the Categories. Kant thought that there must be something that links (mediates between) sensible intuition and understanding. When we make a judgment, say in the form S is P, the subject is a particular sensuously intuited under the *a priori* forms of Space and Time, while the predicate is a general concept expressing our understanding of what is intuited, which concept is possible in terms of the Categories. In order for the Categories to yield concepts applicable to spatio-temporal objects, they must somehow be connected with Space and Time. This connection is called schematizing and is accomplished, according to Kant, by the Imagination. What precisely this means and whether it is internally coherent is a matter of dispute among Kantian scholars. Fortunately, it is not necessary for us to pursue the matter further. The point worth remembering is that, since Kant could not abstract forms from physical objects and yet had to attribute forms to physical objects in thinking those objects, he had to find some way of getting the forms into space and time. In a sense he had the opposite problem from the Aristotelian. Aristotle had to find a way for the mind to drop out material conditions from concepts, while Kant has to find a way to join concepts to material conditions.

Lonergan

In *Insight* Lonergan too attempts to do justice to the *a priori*.[8] Just as Kant tried to establish the Categories of the Understanding by a "deduction," so Lonergan too makes a move similar to Kant's Transcendental Deduction, although Lonergan attempts to deduce the *a priori* conditions of possibility of a judgment of fact rather than the conditions of possibility of our knowing an *object* (as Kant did). Lonergan asks what makes such an *act* of cognition possible; Kant asks what makes the *object* of cognition possible. Hence, one might expect different results.

Let us consider Lonergan's deduction and then compare it to Kant's. If there is any judgment of fact, it consists formally in a "yes" or "no" answer to the question "Is it so?" Such an answer is absolute in that the possible answers are mutually exclusive. Such an answer is rational in that it depends upon evidence. But an answer that is rational and absolute must depend upon grasping an unconditioned. Finally, a judgment of fact does not concern what *must* be but simply what is, and so the unconditioned is not formally but only virtually so. Hence, the first *a priori* condition of a judgment of fact is the *grasp of the virtually unconditioned*.

But before one can answer "yes" or "no" to the question "Is it so?" one must understand the conditioned (the proposition to be affirmed) and the link to its conditions. Hence, prior to answering the question for reflection, one must have answered the question for intelligence, "What is it?" But the answers to questions for intelligence suppose the positing of systematic unities and relations as hypotheses. These are hypotheses and not necessities; otherwise, the answer to "Is it so?" would always be "yes," and then there would be no judgment of fact. At the same time there must be some reference of the conditioned to the field of fulfilling conditions, because otherwise one could never tell whether or not the conditions are fulfilled and so again judgment of fact would be impossible. The second *a priori* condition is an act of intelligence which positions systematic unities with reference to a field of fulfilling conditions, but not such that those conditions are necessarily fulfilled.

Finally, this second condition supposes still another. There must be a field of fulfilling conditions or, better, there must be a field of data (givens) which can become fulfilling conditions once a conditioned has been proposed for judgment. But the field of data which can become fulfilling conditions must function for the particular judgment of fact as a concrete possibility. But for the possibility to be concrete the data must be brought together into existential unity and so must be manifested as a unity-identity-whole of the data, that is, as having been given as a "thing," a first substance in Aristotle's sense of existing individual. Suppose the question arises "Is a gold mountain possible?" Before one can answer "yes" or "no," one would have to seek out sufficient evidence. But to seek out the evidence one would have to understand the question. The question might mean simply "Is there any logical contradiction involved?" and an answer might be "I don't see any." But, of course, that is not satisfactory because one's failure to see a contradiction does not imply that there is none. Hence, the question comes down to one of concrete possibility, and we know what procedure would settle the question (even if we could not carry it out). Get enough gold to constitute a mountain; bring it together in one place (to form a unity-identity-whole: "this mountain"); observe whether it remains in existence for some specified interval of time. If it does, a gold mountain is possible; otherwise, not.

The *a priori* for Lonergan, then, is neither a set of forms of sensibility nor a set of categories of the understanding. The *a priori* is the immanent structure of human intelligence itself. As such, it articulates the Scholastic maxim "Whatever is received is received according to the capacity of the receiver." That capacity is spelled out as the invariant structure of knowing any object at all: presentation, understanding, judgment.

Lonergan puts the contrast between his and Kant's deduction as follows:[9]

1. Kant attempts to deduce the conditions of possibility of something being an *object* of knowledge; Lonergan attempts to deduce the conditions of possibility of the *act* of judging a matter of fact. The point seems to be that Kant assumes that the notion of "being an object" and of "objectivity" is clear enough to support a deduction of their possibility; while Lonergan thinks that it is precisely those notions which need to be clarified in terms of the acts of cognition which posit them. Hence, he looks for the conditions of possibility of those acts and from the structure of intelligence thus discovered goes on to explicate "objectivity" in terms of what is intelligently understood and rationally affirmed.[10]

2. Kant sharply distinguishes between phenomenon and noumenon; Lonergan distinguishes thing-for-us and thing-itself. Each of these is a move away from the primary/secondary sense qualities of Locke. Kant recognized correctly that if Locke is right at all about our knowing our ideas, then both primary and secondary qualities are appearances and so phenomenal (formally mind-dependent). Hence, objectivity requires something else, the noumenon or thing-in-itself, which unfortunately cannot be

known! Lonergan's distinction is neither Lockean nor Kantian. It is simply that between two acts of cognition: description and explanation.

3. Kant is especially interested in necessary judgments (synthetic *a priori*); Lonergan is especially concerned with judgments of fact because they add to our knowledge of the world and provide the way in which one can move from merely analytic propositions to analytic principles (the counterpart of Kant's necessary judgments).

4. Kant grounds judgment immediately in the schematism of the categories; Lonergan grounds it in the grasp of the virtually unconditioned. Since Kant is concerned about the possibility of knowing an object, he thinks he must link the categories with the forms of sensibility. So, for example, the category "Real" is properly used if there is a filling of the empty form of Time. "Substance" is properly used if there is permanence of the Real in Time, etc. Lonergan is concerned about the structure of the act of judging a matter of fact and finds it in the fact that the virtually unconditioned makes possible the absolute "yes" or "no." Kant banishes the unconditioned to the Ideal of Pure Reason and labels any claim to having grasped it as a transcendental illusion. For Kant the unconditioned is not constitutive of knowing an object; it is merely a regulative ideal. For Lonergan the unconditioned is prior to and constitutive of an affirmation of the virtually unconditioned.

5. Kant recognizes at the level of experience only empirical consciousness, that is, the awareness concomitant with acts of perceiving, imagining, judging, etc. He deduces the unity of apperception as the *a priori* condition of possibility of all cognition, that is, the "I think." Lonergan recognizes at the level of experience consciousness as polymorphic, that is, as aware not only of the empirically given but also of the acts of understanding and of reflection which generate both all concepts and systems and all grasp of the virtually unconditioned. Recognizing those acts in conscious experience allows the deduction of the *a priori* structure of mind which makes those acts possible.

Finally, to neglect the role of conceptual frameworks in our understanding of things is to sacrifice the role of culture, history, learning, and system in our account of human knowing. To this we must now turn our attention.

Notes

1. *Metaphysics*, 980A22.
2. The questions are reflected in each of his three critical works: *The Critique of Pure Reason* (What can I know?), *The Critique of Practical Reason* (What ought I to do?), and *The Critique of Judgment* (What can I hope for?).
3. See P. Rousselot, *The Intellectualism of Saint Thomas*, trans. J. Mahony (London: Sheed & Ward, 1935); J. Maréchal, *Le Point de départ de la métaphysique* V, 2nd ed. (Brussels: L'Edition Universelle, 1949); Lonergan, *Insight*, passim.
4. Lonergan, *Insight*, pp. 87–89.
5. See Immanuel Kant, *Critique of Pure Reason*, trans. Norman Kemp Smith (New York: St. Martin's, 1961), passim.
6. See Lonergan, *Verbum*, pp. 141–81 for an excellent treatment of abstraction in Aquinas.
7. Kant, *Critique*, "The Transcendental Analytic." See H. J. Paton, *Kant's Metaphysic of Experience* I (London: Allen & Unwin, 1936), pp. 239ff.
8. See Lonergan, *Insight*, passim, but especially pp. 336–39 for his "transcendental deduction" of the *a priori*.
9. Ibid., pp. 339–42.
10. For Lonergan's treatment of "objectivity," see *Insight*, chap. 3, pp. 375–84.

Study Questions

1. What is the only thing that would completely satisfy our drive to know?
2. What is understood by the horizon of inquiry? What determines our choice of one or more such horizon?
3. What are some of the important implications of the unrestricted desire to know for understanding ourselves?
4. Give two basic models of abstraction. Why is the "impoverished replica" model incorrect?
5. What is the "Kantian turn" in philosophy? Was Kant the first philosopher to realize the active role of the subject in knowing?
6. Sketch Kant's position concerning the role of the *a priori* in knowing (sensibility and understanding).
7. What did Kant mean by saying that all knowledge arises with

experience but not all knowledge arises from experience?

8. Why did Kant say that Space and Time are intuited rather than thought?

9. For Kant, what was the relation of sensuous intuitions to concepts?

10. Why did Kant think he needed the schematism of the categories?

11. How would you understand this claim: Kantianism is an attempt to account for knowing without Aristotelian abstraction?

12. Give an account of Lonergan's transcendental deduction of the conditions of possibility of a judgment of fact.

13. How does Lonergan see his deduction as different from Kant's?

8

Complementing the Classical View: Truth, Error, and Conceptual Frameworks

PERHAPS ONE OF THE MOST IMPORTANT and perplexing issues in contemporary philosophy is the nature and role of conceptual frameworks. What one thinks of this matter impinges upon what one will say on a host of other matters. How one thinks of conceptual frameworks will influence one's theory of meaning; how one thinks concepts are formed; whether one is able to distinguish conceptual relativity from relativism; how one understands conceptual and cultural pluralism. All these are extremely relevant questions in our age of mass and instantaneous communications. It is no longer a matter of whether we choose to face these problems; it is a matter of whether we will face them intelligently or not.

CONCEPTUAL FRAMEWORKS

Let us see whether we can grasp what is meant by a conceptual framework. As a first approximation we might say that it is a point of view or perspective on reality.[1] A particular point of view is determined by a matrix of concepts which we use to order our experience and to orient our responses to the world. Insofar as such a matrix is expressed linguistically it is called a linguistic framework. Frequently frameworks are the result of cultural and historical development and include the attitudes and values of particular groups of people (a people's ethos). Frameworks can be more specialized, however, and can form a sub-framework within a broader cultural network. For example, modern science in its investigation of the world is one vast and complex conceptual framework defined by certain canons of empirical method. Again, Euclidean geometry is a framework within which to interpret space. There are other, non-Euclidean, geometries each of which is another framework within which also to interpret space. In these cases the framework is determined by the axioms of the geometry.

Our characterization of a conceptual framework is indeed informal and imprecise, but it is perhaps sufficient for our present purposes. Those purposes are: (1) to acquaint the reader with several difficult problems (without resolving them); (2) to say a few things to help avoid the trap of relativism; and (3) to consider in what ways different frameworks might be related.

First, there are at least two problems which Wilfrid Sellars has identified and to which he has offered solutions radically different from those of the "tradition."[2] The first has to do with meaning; the second, with concept formation. For the most part, according to Sellars, the "tradition" has held a Concept Empiricism. Such empiricism treats meaning as fundamentally a *relation* between the words of a given language and objects in the physical world. On this understanding of meaning, "red" means the red physical objects to which that word and concept have been associated. The German word *"rot"* has the same meaning as "red" because *"rot"* is related to the very same red physical objects as "red" is. Ultimately this theory of meaning is based on ostensive definition. This theory is unsatisfactory for several reasons, among which is that ostensive definition cannot account for logical connectives like "and," "or," "not," "if . . . then. . . ." Furthermore, he argues that words do not have meaning except *within* a linguistic-conceptual framework. The framework is not built up from pieces; rather, the pieces have meaning from the whole framework. Thus, to say that *"und"* means "and" is to say that the function of *"und"* in the linguistic framework of German is the same as that of "and" in English. "'*Rot*' means red" does not mean simply that both *"rot"* and "red" are related to red physical objects (even though this is true) but rather that *"rot"* functions within the framework which is German in identically the way as "red" functions within English. If this analysis is correct, another problem immediately arises for Concept Empiricism: namely, it is no longer plausible to say that concepts are formed by abstraction from some pre-conceptual sensible awareness and that a conceptual framework is built up piecemeal from such abstractions. Rather, concepts come in bunches—in whole systems of them—and it is only in learning the system that we are able to understand individual concepts (taken in abstraction from the system).

We cannot here examine this alternative view to the classical theory of abstraction as we presented it in the chapter on conceptualization. It does deserve careful thought and critical review. With regard to avoiding the trap of relativism while at the same time taking the role of conceptual frameworks seriously, perhaps the follow reflections will be helpful.[3] First, all human truths must be expressions having meaning, and so they can be expressed in some conceptual-linguistic framework or other. It is from those frameworks that our meanings are understood—from *within* the framework. This means knowing the rules of the particular "language game." There is no expression of truth which transcends all frameworks. There is no universal and unchanging expression of truth.

Second, expressions in different frameworks cannot, as they stand, be compared; hence, they can be said neither to agree nor to disagree. For any comparison to be possible both must be translated into some common and more inclusive framework. This may not always be easy or even possible. Before we can agree or disagree with some statement, we have to make sure that we are working within the same framework. It follows then that it makes no sense to say that what is true in one framework may be false in another. As long as they are in different frameworks they cannot be compared at all, and if and when they are translated into a common framework, then they are either true or not, compatible or not.

Third, conceptual-linguistic frameworks themselves are neither true nor false. They may be more or less powerful, more or less adequate for certain purposes. Only statements within the framework may be true or false.

Fourth, conceptual-linguistic frameworks can and do undergo change in the course of history. Those changes reflect the needs, wants, and desires of the framework users. The frameworks are adapted more adequately to meet those needs sometimes consciously and deliberately, sometimes unconsciously, and almost imperceptibly.

Finally, compatible with these considerations about conceptual-linguistic frameworks is the notion of universal, timeless, and unchanging *truth*. Thus the notion of frameworks does not exclude such truth. For truths are what statements in frameworks express, and there is nothing to prevent a universal truth from being variously and differently expressed. Or to put it another way: it does not follow from the fact that a truth must be expressed in some framework or other that the truth is only that expression. There can be and there are items which are invariant under framework transformation. These are truths some of which may turn out to be universal, necessary, and "eternal." Eternal truths do not require eternal expressions.

Still, conceptual-linguistic frameworks can be compared and related (granted, through the use of a higher, mediating framework). The question arises, then, what the appropriate logic is for expressing the various ways in which frameworks are interrelated. A useful suggestion has been made by Patrick Heelan.[4] While it would take us too far afield to follow his presentation in detail, it is important that you know about this analysis and where you can find more about it.

Here is the gist of Heelan's proposal. He points out that, while statements within an already constituted framework are governed by the usual laws of logic (they are truth-functional, that is, either true or false), when we deal with statements from *different* frameworks, those statements may or may not be simultaneously truth-functional depending upon whether or not those contexts can be realized together at the same time. If they cannot be so realized, the statements are contextually incompatible; if they can, they are simultaneously truth-functional. It is the case of contextual incompatibility which raises the problem since, in general, the descriptive predicates of the incompatible frameworks cannot simply be added together (in the Boolean sense of the union of sets). Heelan suggests that a fruitful model for the logical relations between such frameworks or contexts is a Q-lattice which is non-Boolean and non-distributive. This is a non-classical logic of frameworks rather than of sentences within a framework. (See Appendix II.)

Theories of Truth

In our Introduction we discussed the meaning of the term truth. It would be good to review that material now. There remains the task of considering the classical *theories* of truth. A theory of truth involves not only the meaning of the term but also in general what conditions must be fulfilled for a proposition to be called true. There are three classical theories: (1) the Correspondence Theory, (2) the Coherence Theory, and (3) the Pragmatic Theory.[5] Advocates of any of these theories might admit Tarski's Semantic Conception of Truth as *exhibiting* what they mean by saying that a proposition is true ("p" is true, if and only if p), but they would differ as to what warrants one's assertion of p in the first place. The correspondence theorist would put it in the correspondence or agreement between what is asserted and a fact; the coherentist would put it in the compatibility of what is asserted with other assertions within a system; finally, the pragmatist would put it in the utility or "workability" of what is asserted.

Correspondence Theories

Let us begin with correspondence. In the first place, there is not just one correspondence theory.[6] There are many, and they have in common little more than the claim that the warrant of truth is some sort of similarity in structure between what is asserted (the proposition expressed in a sentence) and a fact (frequently understood to be a non-linguistic state of affairs). If these "correspond," the assertion is warranted; if they do not, it is not.

But in what such correspondence consists is a matter of dispute. Two points have to be clarified: (1) what precisely corresponds to what? and (2) in what does the relation of correspondence consist?

With respect to the first, something has to be said about "what is asserted" and about "fact." Is what is asserted a sentence or a proposition? Behind this question is the issue of whether the sentence "expressing" a proposition is really distinct from the proposition. A thoroughgoing Nominalist would deny such a distinction, while a Conceptualist or Realist might affirm it. If we assume that it is at least plausible to admit such a distinction, then we have to give some account of what a proposition might be (Is it an eternal Platonic entity? Is it a mental act or state? Is it simply the meaning of the sentence expressing it?).[7] Supposing that this part is handled satisfactorily, we still have to say what a fact is. The issue here is whether a fact is a non-linguistic, non-mental entity; and if it is, whether that entity is an event, situation, or state of affairs. We might be tempted to answer quickly that a fact must be non-linguistic and non-mental (in order to escape subjectivism or linguistic idealism). And indeed such a position seems obvious until we reflect that some facts are *negative* and some facts are *general*.[8] It becomes more difficult to posit, for example, what is not the case or what did not happen as an event, situation, or state of affairs. So some have argued that the correspondence between what is asserted and a fact is either a correspondence between two linguistic entities or no correspondence at all since what is asserted and the fact are identical (at least in the case where what is asserted is true).

With respect to the second, something has to be said about the relation called "correspondence." There are at least two ways in which this can be understood: (1) something may correspond *with* something else, or (2) something may correspond *to* something else. "Correspond *with*" has the sense of "fitting" or "agreeing" as a key fits a lock. "Correspond *to*" has the sense of "correlating with," "being in a one-to-one relationship with." Thus it makes sense to say that that-p corresponds *to* the fact that-p; while it does not make sense to say that that-p corresponds *with* the fact that-p. If I say that some physical theory corresponds with the facts, I mean that the theory is consistent with those facts and presumably explains those facts. I surely do *not* mean that the theory corresponds *to* the facts since the theory is more than the facts. In correspondence theories of truth, therefore, "correspondence to" connects that-p and the fact that-p; "correspondence with" connects that-p with other facts (that-p is compatible with them).

Failure clearly to distinguish these relations led the early Wittgenstein, for example, to think of correspondence as a "picturing" relation. He held that a proposition is true if the language in which it is expressed is a picture of the fact meant. It is difficult to give a plausible account of this position since it seems difficult to understand in what way a linguistic reality can be like a non-linguistic reality. Perhaps what he had in mind is that language (here an ideal or perfect language) taken as a physical reality (letters, words, sounds) is perspicuous, that is, literally shows in its structure the structure of the world. Thus, "a is above b" would be written a/b, showing what is meant. If this is at all plausible, that plausibility vanishes when language expresses negative facts, or what is generally or always true, or logical operators. Wittgenstein attenuated his claim saying that he did not mean picturing in the sense that linguistic expression had to look like the facts they expressed, but rather that between them there had to be a similarity of structure, a one-to-one correspondence of linguistic structure *to* the structure of the fact. This would be something like projection in geometry. The trouble with this interpretation of "picturing" is that it has now become so attenuated as to add little or nothing to our understanding of correspondence. This is so, because it can be shown that anything can be projected upon anything.

If the model of "picturing" will not do, what will? In the first place, following White, correspondence is best understood as "correspondence *to*" because this requires no assumption that statements must resemble facts.[9] In the second place, in order to remain faithful to the Aristotelian insight captured by Tarski's formula, it seems sufficient to say simply that a true statement *names both* what it expresses *and* the fact to which it refers. The Scholastics might have put it this way: a statement is true if the intentional relation so expressed conforms to the physical relation experienced and understood.

Coherence Theory

Coherence Theory is rooted in two things: (1) the fact that mathematics and logic are deductive systems whose sole essential characteristic is consistency; and (2) certain rationalistic systems of metaphysics (frequently inspired by mathematics). Because of this twofold source, one finds both Rationalists and Logical Positivists holding this view of truth.

For the Coherentist, the test of a statement's truth is whether it is consistent with a system (a set of compatible propositions). This is a plausible criterion in that we know from logic that if two or more propositions are inconsistent they cannot all be true.

Furthermore, we frequently use as a rule of thumb that, if a claim is made which is inconsistent with either common-sense opinion or with accepted scientific views, it is to be looked upon with suspicion at least. More than that, however, led philosophers to espouse Coherence. Many felt that the difficulties with certain forms of Correspondence could not be overcome so that another theory was required. Since mathematics and logic draw necessary conclusions (and hence, if they are true at all, they are necessarily true), some looked to those disciplines for an understanding of truth. Both mathematics and logic are deductive and systematic. They begin with a set of axioms, and from those axioms theorems are deduced by means of valid argument forms. The only criterion for the truth of a mathematical or a logical statement is consistency with the axioms of the system.

Other philosophers (the Rationalists) transposed the systematic and deductive features of mathematics and logic to the world of actual beings and endowed that world with the property of necessity characteristic of mathematics and logic. In a word, these Rationalists constructed a metaphysics on the model of an axiomatic system. In such a world everything is essentially related to everything else, so that, if anything in that world changes, everything does. This is called the doctrine of *internal relations*. On this view of reality, we do not really know anything unless we know everything. Or, perhaps, better: we do not know anything unless we know it as part of the system. I take it that such was Hegel's view when he declared that truth is in the totality. It follows, of course, that the Coherentist can hold degrees of truth. If the whole truth is found only in the whole system, any individual statement is only part of the truth, and so is only partly true, and so is partly false!

The Coherence Theory remains plausible only as long as one accepts certain views about mathematics and logic, on the one hand, and about internal relations, on the other. Consider mathematics and logic. It is correct to say that both these disciplines have consistency as their essential characteristic. If a mathematical or logical theorem is shown to be inconsistent with its axioms, it is immediately rejected. Hence, it makes sense to say that such theorems are "true" if and only if they are consistent. It follows (correctly, I think) that both Euclidean and non-Euclidean geometries are "true." But when one realizes that neither mathematical nor logical theorems need be about the actual world at all, one sees that Coherence is a very limited theory. If, however, one insisted that it is the only theory of truth, then one would be forced to a skepticism about the truth of matters of fact since matters of fact cannot all be deduced *a priori* from a system's axioms.

Consider the metaphysical doctrine of internal relations. If *all* relations were internal, there would be no distinction between the essential and the accidental, between the relevant and the insignificant. But if this were so, science would be impossible since it could not generalize—every detail would be as significant as every other. Science surely supposes that particular place and particular time are irrelevant to our understanding physical laws. Whether you drop a rock in China or in Brazil makes no difference to the law of gravitation. Furthermore, if all relations were internal, by the slightest movement of my little finger I would change the internal structure of the universe! I find that a little difficult to believe. It may be (and, no doubt, is) the case that some relations are internal, but other relations are merely external and accidental. This is the stuff of which contingent matters of fact are made and of which Coherence fails to give an account.

Finally, it surely is the case that a system can be internally consistent and false. Ptolemaic astronomy seems to be a case in point. World views may be internally coherent but wrong. I can tell a beautifully plausible but fictitious story. If two or more propositions are true, they are coherent; but the converse is not necessarily so.

Pragmatic Theory

Pragmatism is a philosophical movement that began in the United States in the third quarter of the nineteenth century. The term, then, designates a variety of philosophical views all having a family-resemblance but in details quite different. Roughly speaking, the family-resemblance consists in taking intelligence to be a problem-solving faculty, an instrument for coping with life's problems, both practical and theoretical. The major figures in the movement were Charles S. Peirce, William James, and John Dewey.

Among the Pragmatists, James is perhaps the best known for developing it as a theory of truth.[10] Oddly enough, James thought that in so doing he was clarifying the traditional notion of truth as the agreement of an idea with reality. He rejected any "copy" or "picture" theory and replaced it with "workability." An idea agrees with reality if it solves a problem—if it works, if it satisfies our needs, if it forwards our projects and purposes.

Such a pragmatic interpretation of truth has some attractive features that make it plausible. It emphasizes the active role of the knower in seeking out the truth, and provides an attractive alternative to the "spectator" theory of knowledge so vigorously attacked by John Dewey. Pragmatism remains plausible as long as one considers only those cases in which problems are to be solved or an investigation is to be undertaken. It becomes less plausible, however, as soon as one begins to reflect on the difference between accepting something and accepting it as true. Furthermore, there is a difference between something's being *acceptable* as true and something's being true.

All sorts of things (suggestions, plans, excuses, etc.) can be accepted (or rejected) for all sorts of reasons.[11] But something is accepted as true if and only if what is asserted is the case. There is nothing self-contradictory in a falsehood's being useful, satisfactory, or even the solution to a problem. Lies and self-delusion are common enough. Again, something may be acceptable as true without being in fact true. Thus, a scientific hypothesis may be acceptable as true relative to the available evidence, even though in fact it is false (e.g., the geocentric theory of celestial motion). In such cases, the evidence is not sufficient to establish a truth-claim, and the proper judgment would be that the judgment is probable.

The difficulty with Pragmatism in this matter is that it assumes that because we can legitimately expect that true propositions will have consequences which "work," which are "satisfactory," which "advance our purposes," we can also legitimately expect that if a proposition works, satisfies, or advances our purposes, it is true. (Note: we have not even mentioned the problems involved in clarifying what "works," "satisfies," or "advances our purposes" might mean!)

Before leaving the topic of theories of truth, we might usefully consider this question: Must it be that Correspondence,

Coherence, and Pragmatic theories be rivals, and if not, what relation might they have to one another? I suggest two points which might help:

1. There are statements of various kinds: of empirical fact, of scientific theory, of logic and mathematics. I suggest that Correspondence hits off the truth of empirical statements; Pragmatism, the truth of scientific statements; and Coherence, the truth of logical and mathematical statements. Think about the following propositions:

The word processor is gray.

My head aches.

A gas consists of particles (molecules) in motion.

If not not-p, then p.

The interior angles of a triangle equal 180 degrees.

Think about how they might be true. How you answer will involve what you think mathematics, logic, and physical science are about.

2. Perhaps what is right about Coherence and Pragmatism is that they emphasize two important properties of truth as Correspondence. For if a proposition is true in virtue of correspondence, then it is coherent with other true propositions and it has consequences that in some sense are useful and satisfying.

Error

A few words have to be devoted to error. In our Introduction we distinguished error from falsehood. In general, error is affirming what is false or denying what is true. Error arises from a failure to identify evidence correctly, that is, either to think evidence is sufficient when it is not or to think evidence is not sufficient when it is. How can this happen? What are its causes?

Some philosophers have identified the human will as the cause of error. The will, as it were, pushes the intellect to assent "beyond" the evidence. This way of putting the matter is misleading, in that it suggests that will and intellect are two agents within us that act independently of each other and of us. It is rather that we are responsible agents who act through our capacity to know and our capacity to will. Whatever the cause(s) of error might be, they are to be found in the disposition of ourselves as agents.

Among the *occasions* of error (circumstances which make it easy to err) we might mention the complexity and/or obscurity of what we are judging.[12] Among the *causes* of error we might include: (1) one's haste and inattention; (2) one's temerity or boldness; (3) one's confusion resulting from feelings, passions, or emotions; (4) one's prejudices and biases (egocentricity, group loyalty, etc.); and (5) mistakes in reasoning.

It must be clear that one cannot knowingly be in error, even though one's being in error can be culpable and even though knowing that one is in error is not yet necessarily to have discovered the truth. One cannot knowingly be in error, since as soon as one realizes that a certain judgment is erroneous one ceases to believe it. One can be culpably in error if one has failed in the past to take available means to avoid it (e.g., failed to study). To realize that a certain judgment is erroneous and thereby to cease believing it does not always reveal the truth of the matter. It does, however, open one to the possibility of learning. Finally, being in error is not the same as being mistaken. (See Appendix III.)

Notes

1. See Lonergan, *Insight*, pp. 7–19 for the notion of viewpoint.

2. See Sellars, *Science, Perception and Reality* and *Science and Metaphysics: Variations on Kantian Themes* (London: Routledge & Kegan Paul, 1967). For a fine summary of Sellar's position, see C. Delaney, M. Loux, G. Gutting, and W. D. Solomon, *The Synoptic Vision: Essays on the Philosophy of Wilfrid Sellars* (Notre Dame: University of Notre Dame Press, 1977), pp. 1–42.

3. See W. Norris Clarke, S.J., "On Facing up to the Truth about Human Truth," *Proceedings of the American Catholic Philosophical Association*, 43 (1969), 1–12.

4. Patrick A. Heelan, *Space-Perception and the Philosophy of Science* (Berkeley: University of California Press, 1983), pp. 178–91, and pp. 230–42 for a discussion of this formal model applied to the interpretation of rational progress.

5. See, e.g., White, *Truth*, pp. 102–28 for a clear, brief account of these traditional theories.

6. For example, Leibniz held that the correspondence consisted in Pre-established Harmony between the order of knowing and the order of being. Although these orders are parallel and so never interact, God, the author of both, guarantees that our innate knowledge corresponds to (truly represents) what is. Wittgenstein and the Logical Atomists held that correspondence means "picturing." The structure of language is isomorphic to (in one-to-one correlation to) the structure of the world. Finally, the Scholastics, following the Aristotelian tradition, thought of correspondence as conformity of the mind to reality.

7. See ibid., pp. 79–87; see also *Truth*, ed. G. Pitcher (Englewood Cliffs, N.J.: Prentice-Hall, 1964), containing articles by F. D. Ramsey, J. L. Austin, and P. F. Strawson on this matter.

8. See J. O. Urmson, *Philosophical Analysis: Its Development Between the Two World Wars* (Oxford: Clarendon, 1956), esp. pp. 54–93, 141–45 for an account of Logical Positivism's attempt to construct a picturing theory and of the difficulties into which the theory ran.

9. White, *Truth*, pp. 108–109.

10. William James, *Pragmatism* (Cambridge: Harvard University Press, 1975), Lectures II and VI.

11. These criticisms are from White, *Truth*, pp. 125–26.

12. This list of occasions and causes is from Van Steenberghen, *Epistemology*, pp. 174–76; for a more detailed account of bias as a cause of intellectual "blindness," see Lonergan, *Insight*, chaps. 6 and 7.

Study Questions

1. What in general is a conceptual-linguistic framework? Give an example or two.

2. What two problems has Sellars raised for what he called "Concept Empiricism"? What connection have these problems with conceptual frameworks?

3. What does Sellars mean by "Concept Empiricism"? Would he consider our presentation of concept formation (in Chapter 5) such an Empiricism?

4. Can truths be expressed independently of all frameworks?

5. What is necessary before two different frameworks can be compared?

6. Why can frameworks be neither true nor false?

7. Does the fact that frameworks change in the course of history exclude the possibility of unchanging truths?

8. What is Heelan's suggestion for a logic of frameworks?

9. What two key points are a matter of dispute among philosophers who hold a Correspondence Theory of truth?

10. Explain the difference between "correspond with" and "correspond to."

11. What is the "picturing" interpretation of correspondence?

12. Why is "picturing" an unsatisfactory interpretation? What should replace it?

13. In what two things is the Coherence Theory rooted?

14. What is the doctrine of internal relations? How does it lead to the doctrine of degrees of truth?

15. Show that the Coherence Theory is not plausible.

16. What is the Pragmatic Theory of truth and what makes it plausible?

17. What confusions are at work with the Pragmatic Theory?

18. Need the three classical theories of truth be rivals? Explain your answer.

19. List some of the *causes* of error. What might be occasions of error?

20. Can one knowingly be in error? Can one culpably be in error?

9

Memory and Testimony

EVERYONE COMPLAINS OF HIS MEMORY but no one of his judgment. So goes an old saw and with good reason, since memory failure is so common and we seem to have so little control over it. Many times we forget something—our keys, our umbrella, our coat, a poem, a telephone number, historical facts, etc. Sometimes we "remember" something incorrectly or inaccurately. Yet despite the widely admitted fallibility of memory, we rely on it constantly in matters practical and theoretical. If memory were totally unreliable, we could not perform our daily tasks or reason at all (since to draw a conclusion I have to remember the premises!). Hence, in a course about human knowing some attention must be paid to memory, its nature, and its reliability.[1]

Not only do we rely on our own individual memory, but we depend on the memory of others. The remembering of others is reported in their testimony. The question here is: Under what circumstances can we take someone's word for something?

MEMORY

We use the term "remember" in a variety of different but related ways. In fact, this variety of usage is much the same as we already remarked concerning "to know." Thus, we speak of remembering how to do something—drive a car, work a puzzle, play a musical instrument. We also speak of remembering a poem or a speech or the lines of a play. In all these cases of "remembering how to," any challenge to the claim is settled simply by doing the thing in question. Finally, there is a sense of remembering which consists in remembering some fact or event. Usually we express this by "I remember that" such and such happened or "I remember" such and such. Thus I may remember not only how to recite the Pledge of Allegiance but also that I learned it in first grade. These two "rememberings" are quite different, and I can have one without the other. Our analysis of memory will deal only with the sense of "remembering that" since it is a cognitive act which occurs in the present but which is about an event which occurred *in the past*. This cognitive act, moreover, recognizes the event or experience remembered precisely *as in the past*.

We are concerned with two questions: (1) What precisely is it that I directly apprehend when I grasp a past event as past? and (2) Are such apprehensions reliable—that is, is remembering ever a kind of knowing? In general, there are two sorts of answers to the first question. The first is that what is remembered directly is the past event itself. The second is that what is remembered directly is an image of the past event. These positions parallel those discussed in the chapter on sensation—Direct and Indirect Realisms. Let us consider the second answer first.

Image Theory

Many philosophers reject the notion that what is directly remembered is the past event itself on the grounds that the event *is past* and so no longer exists and so cannot be the immediate object of any cognitive act. Furthermore, if what is remembered is the past event itself, how would it ever be possible for one to remember it wrongly or inaccurately? But when we remember a past event, something is present to consciousness. This something is frequently termed an "image" which represents or symbolizes the past event.

The image theory of memory was given classical expression by Hume.[2] Hume held that all knowledge comes from sense experience in the form of images. These images are either impressions or ideas. The difference between them is one of force and vivacity, impressions being more lively and forceful than ideas. Ideas are pale and weak copies of impressions. According to Hume, we can repeat our impressions in either of two ways: the first retains a considerable degree of the vivacity of the original impression and is somewhere in-between an impression and an idea; the second loses that vivacity entirely and is a "perfect idea." The first is called Memory; the second is called Imagination.

For Hume there is a second difference between Memory and Imagination. The more lively images of Memory also preserve the order of the original events, while the less lively images of

Imagination may be put together in any way the creativity of the subject may suggest.

It should be evident that this account will not do. In the first place it labors under the same difficulty as the indirect realisms of perception. If "ideas" (images) are *what* we remember (or perceive), there is no way in which I could ever tell whether the memory (or perception) were veridical since this would involve comparing the ideas (images) with the original. In the second place, one cannot distinguish memory from imagination by claiming that the former preserves the order of the original event without comparing the memory-images with the original impressions of the event. In the third place, memory and imagination cannot always be distinguished by the relative vivacity of whatever images are involved since in fact some imaginings are more vivid than rememberings. Furthermore, what characterizes memory is the *pastness* of the event remembered, and vivacity says nothing at all about that.

Hume's account of memory, then, will not do. Bertrand Russell attempted to remedy the weaknesses in that version of the image theory and put forth an image theory of his own.[3] The first thing to note is that Russell's theory is an image theory and so suffers from the general weakness of Indirect Realism. Instead of distinguishing memory-images from imagination-images in terms of vivacity, Russell introduces the notion of *familiarity*. Memory-images are recognized as memory-images because they are accompanied by the vague feeling "this has happened before" or "I have had this experience before." This provides the element of pastness essential to memory but absent from Hume's vivacity account. There is little doubt that the feeling of familiarity accompanies memories, and a case can be made that the feeling of familiarity has pastness as an element. Thus Russell's memory-images plus a feeling of familiarity do account for our having a notion of pastness, and for our referring some and not other images to the past (as memory does). Still, it is flawed in that it cannot guarantee that any memory is correct. The feeling of familiarity does not entail the notion of correctness or accuracy. For a memory-image which felt familiar to be guaranteed requires that we *know* the remembering to be correct, and whatever evidence we might adduce to support this claim would come from some other remembering; and since, by supposition, all remembering is marked by the feeling of familiarity only, it needs something else to guarantee it.

Direct Realism

The man-in-the-street is convinced that the object of his remembering is the event itself remembered. Some call this "naive" and perhaps justly so, insofar as the man-in-the-street does not critically examine his spontaneous conviction. Perhaps, however, the substance of this conviction can withstand critical examination.

The substance of this position is that *what* we remember is the past event—not an image of it, even if images may play some role in the remembering. The past event is directly present in remembering—not inferred, even though some memories may be filled out or supplemented by inference.

The principal objection to this Direct Realism is that it seems impossible for something that happened in the past to be itself present here and now. The question then is: What evidence do we have that direct acquaintance with a past event (whether in memory or not) is impossible? There is no empirical evidence since it would consist in citing cases where the direct object of remembering was not the object remembered. But, then, what would be the direct object of remembering? An image of the object remembered? But how would one know that the image was of the object remembered unless one directly grasped the object remembered? Whatever evidence is adduced is *a priori* and in particular is a *theory* about the nature of *time*.

But surely, even if it is supposed that it is not impossible for an event that happened in the past to be directly present to consciousness, that event is not present in the same way as it was first perceived. In perception the event was directly present to consciousness as present, as happening now. In memory the event is presented *as past*, as having happened. The role of images or "ideas" in perception is that of media *by which* the event is present. They are *not things* which are known. Similarly, in memory the images involved are not pictures of the past event: they are not *what* is remembered but rather that by which (and perhaps in which) the past event is present to consciousness as past, that is, as remembered.

If we admit this sort of Direct Realism of memory, how could memory ever be incorrect or inaccurate? The problem seems to be that if the past event itself is what is remembered, how could we ever get it wrong? One way around such a difficulty would be to say that in memory we are directly aware of originals of the past event but not necessarily with *the* original. This leaves open the possibility that we confuse two originals, or combine them incorrectly by imagination, or add to or subtract from the originals.

Memory, then, is not always correct and so is not always a mode of knowing. Someone, however, might insist that memory is always correct by definition, that is, unless I remember correctly, I am not really remembering at all. I only *think* I am remembering. One *could* choose to use the term in this way, but it is perhaps more natural to allow that in situations of recalling a past event, I do recall it but incorrectly.

Is memory *ever* a mode of knowing? Unless one is willing to accept skepticism, the answer must be "yes." On the other hand, one must not demand of memory more certitude than one demands of perception itself. One must not demand that memory is to be accepted only if it is necessarily correct. Memory presents us with past (hence, contingent) events, and the propositions based on memory are contingently true. For such a proposition to be accepted as true requires that in it we have grasped the virtually unconditioned. That in some cases at least we do grasp the virtually unconditioned is confirmed both by pragmatic testing of memory and by internal evidence. The internal evidence or data of consciousness concerning memory spring from the fact that memories always imply the self as subject of the experience remembered. Whenever I claim to remember an event, I imply not only that the event is past but also that I once directly experienced it. The pragmatic test of memory is that we use it successfully, for example, to find things and so on. So one might formulate evidence as sufficient for a memory claim as follows:

1. If I have the testimony of consciousness that the event remembered is an event I once witnessed,
2. and if that memory is consistent with and successful in dealing with present experience,
3. then that memory is reliable.

In the case where others remember the same event but perhaps with differences concerning details, there arise problems concerning the degree of accuracy of the memory which can be resolved only if there is some independent way of checking the accounts. This sort of problem arises frequently in testimony.

When we have the experience of remembering something, we actually re-experience ourselves having the first experience. We experience again the event remembered as having been perceived by us. It has those qualities of the original perception (passivity and receptivity of the perceiver, the sense of having gained information, etc.) but not as now perceived or as now actively imagined, but precisely as *recalled*, as drawn out from our inner world. The memory keeps the feeling of a perception (e.g., in an ordered series) but not as going on now. The memory fits into a continuous succession of experiences which were ours in the past and are recognized as ours (this is not generally true of dreams, for example). In other words, we have an awareness of ourselves as perduring identical agents. In remembering we re-experience ourselves as the selfsame agent acting at a particular time and place in this ordered series of *our* experiences. This suggests that our experience forms a spatio-temporal continuum extending into the past which we can explore at will. If something like this is true, we have an alternative to the Hume–Russell model of memory simply as a set of images in the present which then have to be connected somehow with the past. Rather memory-images are already intrinsically connected with our past and so are the means by which we re-experience ourselves experiencing the event remembered.

Before we leave our consideration of memory, a few further remarks are in order:

1. It may be, and frequently is, the case that the further back we go in the space–time continuum of our experience, the more difficult it is to remember clearly and accurately (although sometimes in elderly people the opposite seems to be true).

2. Just as perceptual judgment (perception as formal knowing) has a conceptual as well as sensitive component, so too memory as formal knowledge has a conceptual as well as sensitive component. Thus, some speak of sensitive memory and intellectual memory, where intellectual memory means habitual knowledge of concepts and general truths. When we remember a past

event as past, we also remember what predicates correctly describe it, etc.

3. Very little is known about the relation of memory to brain function, except that damage to certain parts of the cortex inhibits or destroys memory in some cases. Yet it can, and sometimes does, happen that other parts of the brain take over the memory function of the damaged portion. Furthermore, there seems to be no specific correlation between brain function and intellectual memory. It also seems to be well established that the brain does not "store" images, in the sense that there are neural traces on the cortex which correlate with memory-images.

Testimony

Human society could not long operate efficiently and peaceably unless we accepted the testimony of others. Only a tiny fraction of our working "knowledge" and beliefs is the result of personal experience and research. Hence, we do in fact trust others. Is this a rational thing to do and, if so, under what general conditions?

By *testimony* we mean the assertion of something as true by a witness and proposed to someone for belief. Here *belief* means, not just opinion (although, as we have seen, philosophers often use the term in that sense), but accepting something on faith or trust in the *authority* of the one testifying. In the case of testimony, the one who believes the witness does not have sufficient *intrinsic* evidence for the truth of what is believed, and so testimony is sometimes said to be *extrinsic* evidence. Indeed, for accepting testimony as true, there must be some intrinsic evidence, but evidence that directly bears not on what is testified to but rather on the authority of the witness. In other words, in order for one rationally to accept testimony, one must establish the authority of the witness; that is, one must establish by intrinsic evidence that the witness is *competent* in the matter to which he is testifying (he is in a position to know what he is talking about) and that he is *trustworthy* (he is not lying).

Some, following the Cartesian doubt, would argue that testimony is never a source of knowledge, since the witness can always be in error and can lie. Hence, one can never have certitude about any matter on the word of another; hence, one can never gain knowledge except by one's own personal grasp of a "clear and distinct" idea. The vast majority of thinkers, however, hold that sometimes, under certain conditions, testimony is a source of knowledge.

Consider the case where there are *many independent* witnesses testifying to a *public, easily knowable* fact. Witnesses are "independent" in their testimony when they have not conspired to tell the same story, have not gotten their testimony (all or in part) from hearsay, or have any other connection that might influence what they say. Consider two newspaper accounts of an event. One might suppose that they are independent testimony, but if one notices that both are citing Reuters or that both are owned by the same publisher, their independence is destroyed or rendered suspect.

Suppose that truly independent witnesses (many thousands of them) testify from firsthand experience to the existence of a country called China, across the Pacific Ocean, having over a billion people, etc., etc. Such testimony would yield certain knowledge of the fact attested. If their testimony was false, it would be because either they were in error or they were all lying. But for many witnesses to be in error about a readily ascertainable public fact not only is unlikely, it is absurd. For all these witnesses to be deliberately deceiving us is an unreasonable hypothesis precisely because the deception could be so easily discovered. It seems fantastic that none of these thousands would dissent or leak the deception or in some way contradict the claim. The only reasonable explanation of the substantial agreement of witnesses in this case is that they are telling the truth. Without checking out the competence and veracity of each of these thousands of witnesses (an impossible task), the sheer convergence of their testimony is itself evidence for the truth of their witness.

Note that this analysis applies only to cases of public fact readily accessible. It does not apply to facts which are *difficult* to know (e.g., human motives) or to theories, hypotheses, explanations. It would be possible for whole societies to hold erroneous theories for long periods of time. It may be true that widespread agreement about a theory may lend extrinsic support for the theory, that is, force us to take it seriously, but it does not afford evidence for the truth of the theory. In such cases it is frequently difficult to exclude common error (even if we can usually exclude common deception).

What about testimony from a few, or even a single, witness? Is it ever sufficient grounds for certain knowledge of the fact attested to? Under certain conditions, yes. Here the all-important thing is careful investigation of the witness(es)' competence and truthfulness. Now, it seems that in some cases at least, when the fact attested is easily knowable, one could have such personal knowledge of the witness as to have solid reasonable grounds, perhaps even certitude, of the truth of his testimony. In any case, one must be able to exclude all motives the witness may have for lying. One must be aware of emotional, cultural, or personal influences that might vitiate the witness' impartiality and objectivity. None of this is easy; perhaps it is rarely accomplished; but it is possible.

These cursory and elementary considerations about testimony as a source of certain knowledge bear especially on the discipline of history, the legal profession, and religion. When one studies any of these areas, one of the important topics is methodology. A great portion of the methods employed by the historian, the lawyer, and the theologian aim at establishing the authority of witnesses. For example, the historian frequently must use documents as testimony (direct or indirect, explicit or implicit) to past events. Not only must he attempt to determine the competence and truthfulness of the document's author, he must also make sure that the document itself is authentic (not a forgery), is faithful to the original (e.g., trace the manuscript tradition for errors in copying, etc.), is correctly dated, and so on.[4] This requires a great deal of skill and a great deal of learning on the researcher's part. The results frequently are only probable. Again, the lawyer must know the rules of admissible evidence and learn how he may establish or impugn the veracity of a witness (his character, his knowledge, etc.). In theology, since the great Western religions (Judaism, Christianity, and Islam) all claim revelation from God as the ultimate author of their sacred books (Old Testament, New Testament, Koran), a major issue is how to establish that the human author of the book is telling the truth when he claims (implicitly at least) to be passing on something God has revealed to him. To face this issue was the role in theology of what was called "apologetics" as a part of fundamental theology. In this case, the theologian tried to show that accepting the message of the sacred writer as a message from God was *reasonable* (not apodictically certain), usually by examining the internal evidence of the message and the character, personality, and life of the human witness.

Notes

1. This entire discussion of memory is derived from Woolzey, *Theory of Knowledge*, pp. 36–69.
2. *Treatise of Human Nature*, Bk. I, Pt. I, Sec. III; Bk. I, Pt. III, Sec. V.
3. *The Analysis of Mind* (London: Allen & Unwin; New YorK: Macmillan, 1921), Lecture I.
4. See, e.g., Bernard Norling, *Towards a Better Understanding of History* (Notre Dame: University of Notre Dame Press, 1960) for a brief but informative introduction to historical method.

Study Questions

1. How are memory and testimony linked?
2. What are some of the ways in which we use the term "remember," and how especially are we using it in this chapter?
3. What are the two principal questions concerning memory, and what are the two general sorts of answers?
4. How did Hume distinguish Memory from Imagination?
5. Why will Hume's account of memory not do?
6. How did Russell try to correct Hume's account?
7. Why will Russell's account not do either?
8. Simply stated, what does Direct Realism hold concerning memory?
9. What is the principal objection to Direct Realism's account and how is it to be handled?
10. How is the role of memory-images understood in Direct Realism? How does this compare to the role of images in Direct Realism's account of perception?
11. How does Direct Realism account for error in remembering?
12. Is remembering ever a mode of knowing? Under what conditions?
13. How does our awareness of ourselves as agents who exist over a

period of time help us understand memory? How must we think of time on this interpretation?

14. Is there intellectual as well as sensitive memory? Explain.

15. What in general might be said about the function of the brain in memory?

16. What is meant by "testimony"? In the context of testimony does "belief" mean "opinion"? Explain.

17. What is meant by the "authority" of the witness?

18. Why do some philosophers deny that testimony can ever be a source of true and certain knowledge?

19. Discuss the case of many independent witnesses to a public and easily accessible fact.

20. Discuss the case of a few (or even just one) witnesses to a public and easily accessible fact.

21. When historians deal with documents what special problems do they encounter?

22. How might a lawyer apply our general considerations to witnesses in court?

23. What bearing does the question of testimony have upon theologies of revelation?

10

Inference: A Source of Knowledge

IN CHAPTER 3 we introduced the notion of inference and distinguished three kinds: deduction, induction, and abduction. It would be good to review that material in order to follow more closely the discussion in this chapter concerning inference as a source of knowledge.

DEDUCTION: NEW KNOWLEDGE?

Concerning deductive inference, the standard attack against it as a source of knowledge is that the conclusion is already in the premisses and so tells us nothing new. Consider the following. The conclusion of a sound deductive argument is *guaranteed* to be true. A deductive argument is said to be *sound* if two conditions are met: (1) the argument form is valid, and (2) the premisses are true. Hence, a deductive argument may be valid but unsound (if any one of the premisses is false). In this case, the conclusion is *not* guaranteed to be true; in fact, it might be false. An invalid deductive inference is always unsound (even if the premisses are all true). If one were to ask why the conclusions of sound deductions are necessarily true, the answer is to be found in the fact that the conclusion merely makes explicit what was implicit in the conjunction of the premisses. Hence, it seems, As John Stuart Mill maintained, that deduction is not a source of knowledge; the conclusion merely states what we already know from the premisses.[1]

The problem here revolves around what one means by "new" knowledge. It is correct that the conclusion of a sound deductive argument does not contain any information, any new facts, which were not already in the premisses. Still, there is a sense in which the conclusion adds something to the premisses, since it makes formally explicit what was only implicit in the conjunction of the premisses. Furthermore, the conclusion can be drawn only from the *conjunction* of the premisses. It cannot be drawn from only one of the premisses. Thus, for example, from the conjunction of these premisses:

> All M's are P;
>
> All S's are M;
>
> Hence, all S's are P.

But if we had only one of the premisses, the conclusion would not follow. Thus, from

> All M's are P

no conclusion can be drawn concerning the relation of S to P. Similarly, from

> All S's are M

no conclusion can be drawn concerning the relation of S to P. The conclusion is said to be in each of the separate premisses *virtually* (not *formally*); that is to say, each premiss has the power to yield the conclusion *in conjunction with* the other premiss. In a word, it is the *conjunction* of the premisses which makes the conclusion to be formally but only implicitly present in the premisses. The conclusion merely states explicitly what the premisses taken together imply.[2]

Is this "new" knowledge? Surely not, in the sense that it yields new factual information about the world. And it is true that no matter of contingent fact can be established by deduction alone. Still, there is a sense in which this is "new" knowledge, because, after all, deduction can make a significant addition to the state of my knowledge: namely, to render formally known what was only virtually known in each premiss. Deductive reasoning consists in the bringing together of premisses; the conclusion merely explicitly states what is in the conjunction of the premisses.

Sometimes it is argued that deduction does not give knowledge because it depends upon analytic propositions, that is, upon mere tautologies. I think perhaps the difficulty here is in the "mere." That analytic propositions are in a technical sense "trivial" does not mean that they are useless or superfluous. They, in fact, set the upper bound for true propositions, while contradictions set their lower bound. Furthermore, insofar as the partial terms of meaning which make up the necessary relation expressed in an analytic proposition are instantiated in judgments of fact, the analytic proposition becomes an analytic principle (with existential import). Hence, principles of logic may also be principles of being.

Induction: Certain Knowledge?

In general, inductive argument goes from particular instances to general conclusions. This characterization is not quite accurate, since it also applies to abductive inference. For our purposes it is close enough. Let us say, then, that induction is a case of sampling a set of items or a population to verify some general hypothesis or other about that set or population. Notice that we leave out of consideration "complete induction" or simple enumeration, since this is not a case of inference at all, but rather a case of counting. We also leave out so-called "mathematical induction," since again this is not an induction at all; it is a deduction and as such its conclusion is necessary.[3]

We are concerned with what is called "incomplete induction", that is, where a limited number of cases are examined. What has vexed philosophers for a long time is how to justify drawing a general conclusion from a sample. Are such conclusions ever certain? If they are not certain, in what sense do we know them? In other words, the question raised by induction is just the opposite of that raised by deduction. It seems that deductive conclusions are certain but not new; inductive conclusions are new but not certain.

Let us consider John Stuart Mill's position. He held that induction is the only "real" inference precisely because it gives "new" knowledge; that is, its conclusion contains something not in the premises (i.e., a *general* conclusion from a particular sample or samples). Deduction, for Mill, is not "real," because its conclusion does not contain anything not in the conjunction of the premises (and for that reason the conclusion is certain). Mill, then, was most eager to justify inductive or "real" inference. He tried to do so by appealing to the uniformity of nature. Nature is ordered; it is governed by certain laws; hence, we know that the future will resemble the past and that a sample can be representative of an entire population.[4] Now, if Mill's argument were sound, induction would be justified, because it can be reduced to a deduction whose major premiss is "Nature is uniform." But then Mill would justify "real" inference by reducing it to "unreal" inference. Embarrassing as that might prove to be for Mill, it is not the most important difficulty in his justification of induction. The appeal to the uniformity of nature is viciously circular since the only way in which we could know anything at all about nature and its regularity is by induction. But then, Mill's argument justifying induction depends upon the use of induction.

A sounder and more sophisticated approach to the problem of "justifying" induction is to deny that it needs any justification.[5] First, induction is *not* the process of inference whereby we generalize from particulars. Rather, induction is a process whereby we verify a generalization already made and adopted as an hypothesis. Hence, to ask how many cases we need to have in order to justify a generalization is to put the question poorly. The proper question is, rather: What degree of confirmation does an induction, carried out in a certain way, give to the hypothesis under consideration? This no doubt raises many thorny questions, but it does not raise the issue of justifying induction. Induction, then, is a *process* of verification. If that process is persevered in, any error in the hypothesis being tested must, in the long run, come to light and so be eliminated. Hence, induction is said to be self-correcting and, as self-correcting, self-authenticating in the long run. In the short run, however, no induction can guarantee that the hypothesis is totally error-free.

Consider what happens in induction. Say that I am in the business of buying grain. I know that I can make a profit only if the grain I buy is at least 60% A-quality. When I am considering buying a particular shipment, I must estimate whether at least 60% of the grain is A-quality. I do that by taking samples, and averaging out the results so yielded. Now, everything depends on how those samples were collected. The samples must be at once truly representative of the grain in the shipment under examination *and* truly randomly gathered. The first requirement, that the samples be representative, requires (1) that prior to any actual examination of the grain, I stipulate in advance (pre-designate) what counts as A-quality, (2) that samples be gathered from various parts of the shipment to ensure that I have not picked only from the best or from the worst (say, what was damaged by water or rats or whatever) grain. The second requirement, randomness of the sample, requires that the way in which each sample is gathered is such that any morsel of grain in the area from which the sample is taken has as much chance of being chosen as any other. If these directions for picking representative and randomly chosen samples are carefully followed, the very process itself guarantees that it will discover any errors. For insofar as the samples chosen are truly representative and truly random, that sample is any member of the group you like; hence, what is true of it is true of any member of the group, and what is true of any member of the group is true of every member of the group.[6]

Though most philosophers are unwilling to maintain that scientific method yields certainties, still there are some. An obvious candidate would be those who hold an Aristotelian view of natures and of abstraction. If one accepts the view that things have natures that, in some cases at least, are known by abstraction, then induction is not a problem. Ontologically, the uniformity of nature is guaranteed by the metaphysics of matter and form. Form is grasped by abstraction. The problem is that this seems to be rather like Little Jack Horner and his pie. This is too simple. We are aware that whatever we know about reality has been hard won through persistent investigation and frequent modification of hypotheses. But the neo-Aristotelians are not alone.[7] There are some rationalists who maintain that there is no distinction between the necessary and the contingent. Thus all truths are necessary, and hence there is no problem of induction (indeed, there is no induction at all, in the sense of generalization from experience). Besides the rationalists, certain analysts try various ingenious ways of getting certainty into inductive conclusions. The reason for their attempts is the conviction that knowledge implies the logical necessity of what is known. Furthermore, science is the model of knowing; hence, the conclusions of science must be certain, in the sense of necessary. In my opinion this is just a mistake. It is not necessary to promote the conclusions of science to the status of absolutely certain truths, for those conclusions to be acceptable and accepted. These conclusions would be known in the strict sense (justified true belief) if the evidence supporting these were sufficient. We do have sufficient evidence in countless judgments of fact upon which science rests its conclusions and which make those conclusions truly probable (see Chapter 6 above).

Abduction: Mere Guessing?

We have already mentioned that, strictly speaking, induction does not generalize but rather verifies generalizations already made and used as explanatory hypotheses. What, then, is the process of generalization and of hypothesis formation? It is the third distinct form of inference identified by Peirce.[8] Abduction is the process of inferring a case from a rule and a result (see p. 54 above):

> All the beans in that bag are black.
> These beans are black.
> Hence, (probably) these beans are from that bag.

An hypothesis (an explanation) is required when we find some surprising or curious circumstance (here, that *all* the beans are black), which would be explained by the supposition that it was a case (the beans were in that bag) of a certain general rule (all the beans in that bag are black). "Explanation" means the assertion of some positive matter of fact, other than the fact to be explained, but from which this fact necessarily follows.[9] But what is it about the rule and result which calls for an explanation in terms of the one being a case of the other? In other words, how do we know when an explanation is needed? Surely an explanation is required when questions arise; but questions arise when we encounter the unexpected, that is, when experience surprises us. If experience were perfectly chaotic (no regularity or pattern to it at all), no question about it could arise since nothing would be surprising—literally anything at all might occur. Again, if experience were perfectly regular in its patterns, no question about it could arise since there would be no surprises—all our expectations would always be satisfied. In general, then, the following situations call for an explanation: (1) empirically observed regularities in nature, because they are the exception to the preponderance of experience; and (2) breaches in empirically observed regularities, since the regularity has led one to expect certain phenomena. When they fail to happen, questions arise.[10]

There is a third case needing explanation, namely, failure to discover empirical confirmation of a postulated regularity. Here, what is to be explained is not lack of confirmation, but why one postulated the regularity in the first place.

To answer our question, then, rule and result require an explanation because of an observed regularity, namely, that all the beans on the table are black. If they had been all different colors, no question about their color would have arisen. But the regularity calls for an explanation. If those beans had been drawn from the bag containing only black beans, that itself would be a positive matter of fact and would entail the fact that the beans on the table are black. This is abductive inference.

According to Peirce, for an abductive inference to lead to a probable result, the following guidelines need to be followed: (1) the hypothesis should be distinctly put as a question *before* making the observations that are to test its truth; this corresponds to the pre-designation of characters required for a good induction; (2) the respect in regard to which the resemblances are noted must be taken at random; and (3) failure as well as successes in predictions must be noted.[11]

SOME RULES OF DEDUCTIVE INFERENCE

Only deductive inferences can be said to be valid or not. The reason is this: validity means that it is *necessarily* true that if the premisses are true the conclusion is true. But only deductive inferences have conclusions that follow *necessarily* from their premisses. Induction and abduction, then, are not valid or invalid, but rather warranted or not, well done or not, depending on whether those inferences were carried out according to certain guidelines. Only deductive inferences have rules for validity. The study of these rules is the particular province of Formal Logic. In case the reader has not yet studied this discipline, the following will given him an idea of what valid deductive inference looks like and perhaps will encourage him to take up Logic in earnest.

Immediate Inference

The first important form of deductive argument is that which draws its conclusion from a single premiss. Most logic books call this Immediate Inference because, unlike deductive arguments in the form of the categorical syllogism (which we will consider shortly and at some length), there is no "middle term" uniting the minor and major terms and thus allowing the conclusion to be drawn.

The two most important immediate deductive inferences are (1) those coming from the *Square of Opposition* and (2) those coming from various ways of transforming propositions by *Conversion* and by *Obversion*. Both these groups of immediate inferences obtain between categorical propositions.

Categorical propositions can be affirmative or negative. Furthermore, their subject and predicate terms can be quantified ("all," "some," "exactly one"). In general, there are four kinds of categorical propositions:

> A: Universal Affirmative (All X is Y);
> E: Universal Negative (No X is Y);
> I: Particular Affirmative (Some X is Y);
> O: Particular Negative (Some X is not Y).

Let us explore the relationships these propositions have to one another in virtue of "immediate inference."

(*a*) The Square of Opposition • The four categorical propositions, A, E, I, and O, can be arranged in a square or rectangle for the purpose of illustrating how they "oppose" or negate one another. This "square" of opposition looks something like this:

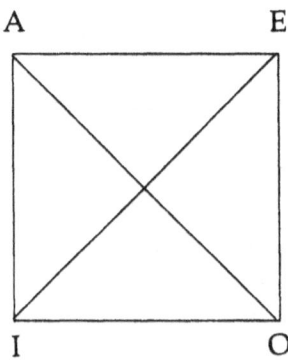

(1) *Contradictories*: A and O, E and I are related as *contradictories*; that is, each is the minimum required to render the other false. Thus, if I am given that A is true, then it follows necessarily that O is false. Again, if I am given that A is false, then it follows necessarily that O is true. In other words, contradictories cannot both be true or both be false. If one is true, the other is false.

(2) *Contraries*: A and E are related as *contraries*, that is, each is the maximum negation of the other. Hence, if I am given that one of them, say A, is true, then it necessarily follows that E is false. But if I am given that one of them is false, then the other may be true or false. In general, contraries cannot both be true, but they can both be false. Consider, if it were true that all men are college graduates, then, of course, it would be false that no men are college graduates. But if it is false that all men are college graduates, it does not follow that it is true that no men are college graduates—in fact, some are, and some are not. Hence A and E can *both* be false, but they cannot both be true.

(3) *Sub-contraries*: I and O are related as *sub-contraries* (under the "contraries" in the diagram!), that is, both cannot be false, although *both* can be true. Thus, if it were false that some man is a college graduate, it would follow necessarily that some man is not a college graduate. But if it is true that some man is a college graduate, then it may be true or it may be false that some man is not a college graduate. Thus I and O cannot both be false, but both can be true.

(4) *Subalterns*: A and I, E and O are related as *subalterns*, that is, as universal to particular. If the universal is given as true and if the universal is not any empty class (i.e., a class with no members, like, say, the class of Martians), then it follows necessarily that the particular is true. One may not, however, go from the truth of the particular to the truth of the universal (even though, under appropriate circumstances, such an inference would be a good *induction*, it is *always* an invalid deduction). Again, given that the classes are not empty, from the falsity of the particular we can validly infer the falsity of the universal. If it is false that some man is a college graduate, then it is also false that all men are college graduates.

You have noticed that in this treatment of the square of opposition it has been assumed that classes with which we were dealing were not empty. Suppose now that we dropped this restriction and allowed empty classes; what would this do to the relations in the square of opposition? I leave the answer for the reader to figure out (or for the instructor to present).

(*b*) Conversion and Obversion • Conversion is an inference whereby a proposition, S is P, is altered so that P and S are switched (P is S) without changing the proposition's quality (i.e., an affirmative remains affirmative and a negative remains negative) or truth-value. Consider the following cases:

(1) "No S is P" can be simply converted to "No P is S," because, since not a single S is a P, not a single P is an S.

(2) "Some S is P" can be simply converted to "Some P is S," since, because there is at least one S which is also P, there must be at least one P which is also S.

(3) "All S is P," however, *cannot* be simply converted to "All P is S," for while it is true that all cats are animals, it is false that all animals are cats. The reason why this sort of conversion is invalid is to be found in the quantity of P in each of those propositions. In the first, where P was in the predicate place, its quantity was particular (some P), while in the second its quantity is universal (all P). Such a move is unwarranted. "All S is P" can be converted to "Some P is S," since here P's quantity is not extended. (Note: the predicate of an affirmative proposition is *always* particular.)

(4) "Some S is not P" simply *cannot* be converted at all. The reason is that the predicate of a negative proposition is *always* universal; but, then, whenever S, the subject of an O proposition, is made its predicate, it becomes universal, thus extending its quantity illegitimately.

Summary of Conversion:

1. E to E and I to I — O.K.
2. A to I — O.K.; NEVER A to A
3. NEVER CONVERT AN O.

Obversion is that inference whereby the quality of a proposition is changed without changing either its quantity or its truth-value. This is done by changing the quality of the given proposition and by replacing its predicate with the complement of that class. Thus, "All men are college graduates" becomes "No man is a non-college graduate." These are all valid obversions:

> A to E: All S is P to No S is non-P.
> E to A: No S is P to All S is non-P.
> I to O: Some S is P to Some S is not non-P.
> O to I: Some S is not P to Some S is non-P.

By using conversion and obversion in different combinations, other inferences can be generated. Here is one frequently used in logic books: contraposition. It is the successive use of obversion, conversion, and obversion again. For example, "All S is P" becomes "No S is non-P" (obversion), which in turn becomes "No non-P is S" (conversion), which finally becomes "All non-P is non-S" (obversion). Try this with the other categorical propositions. Be careful of the I proposition! There is a hidden pitfall in trying to obvert it.

Mediate Inference

Deductive arguments which are not immediate inferences are expressed in *syllogisms*. A syllogism has two premisses and one conclusion. A syllogism may be categorical, hypothetical, or disjunctive.

(*a*) Categorical Syllogisms • A categorical syllogism is made up of categorical propositions, that is, propositions of the form: S is (is not) P. Besides the conclusion, there is a major and a minor premiss. The major premiss is that containing the major term, and the minor premiss is that containing the minor term. The major term is the *predicate* of the conclusion; while the minor term is the *subject* of the conclusion. The term that is common to both premisses is called the *middle* term. A typical form of categorical syllogism is the following:

> M (Middle Term) is P; (Major premiss)
> S is M (Middle Term); (Minor premiss)
> S (Minor Term) is P (Major Term) (Conclusion).

The principle at work in the categorical syllogism is that of class inclusion-exclusion. We can grasp why the above syllogism is valid (that is, if its premisses are true, its conclusion *must* be true). The major premiss says that all M's are included in the class of P's; the minor says that all S's are included in the class of M's;

hence all S's must be included in the class of P's. Consider this negative syllogism:

> No M is P;
> S is M;
> Hence no S is P.

Again, it is class inclusion-exclusion that makes this valid: since not a single M is a P and every single S is an M, it must be that not a single S is a P.

For a categorical syllogism to be valid, all the following rules must be satisfied (if even one of them is violated, the inference is invalid):

(1) The middle term must be distributed (used universally) at least once; otherwise we would get an inference like this: All cats are animals; All dogs are animals; Hence, all dogs are cats!

(2) No term in the conclusion can be used universally unless it was so used in the premisses; otherwise we would get an inference like this: Every Frenchman is a European; No Hungarian is a Frenchman; Hence, no Hungarian is a European!

(3) Two negative premisses yield no conclusion at all.

(4) If the conclusion is negative, there must be one, and only one, negative premiss.

A fifth rule should be added concerning the existential import of universal premisses. The point is that universal propositions do not suppose that there exist any individuals in the classes they use. Thus "All dinosaurs are cold-blooded" does not imply that there exist any dinosaurs. It says simply, "Pick anything at all in the universe; if what you pick turns out to be a dinosaur, than it will also be cold-blooded." On the other hand, if one supposes (as Aristotle did) that none of the classes used in discourse is empty, then this fifth rule is not necessary.

(b) Hypothetical Syllogisms • The major premiss of a hypothetical syllogism is an implication, that is, an "if . . . , then . . . " statement. The minor premiss either affirms the antecedent (the "if" clause) or denies the consequent (the "then" clause), and draws the conclusion, affirming the consequent in the first case, or denying the antecedent in the second.

Thus there are two and only two valid forms of hypothetical inference:

(1) *Modus Ponens*: if p, then q;
but p;
hence, q.

(2) *Modus Tollens*: if p, then q;
~q;
~p.

All other forms are invalid. They are, respectively, the fallacy of positing the consequent and the fallacy of denying the antecedent. Let p be "It is raining," and q be "The streets are wet." Try these in the valid forms and then in the invalid forms. Do you see why they are invalid?

(c) Disjunctive Syllogism • A disjunctive syllogism is valid in one and only one case: namely, where the disjunction is complete, that is, where the disjuncts exhaust the possibilities, and where one can eliminate all but one of the alternatives. Thus,

Either p, or q, or r;
But ~p, and ~q;
Hence, r.

Notes

1. Perhaps the best-known critic of deduction is John Stuart Mill in his *System of Logic* (London, 1843). According to Mill, there is "real" inference only when the conclusion is not already contained in the premises. Hence, only induction is "real" inference. But when Mill attempts to "justify" induction, he does so by reducing it to a form of deduction through an appeal to the "uniformity of nature" as its major premiss.

2. This understanding of how and in what sense deduction yields "new" knowledge is standard among Scholastic philosophers: see, e.g., O'Neill, *Theories of Knowledge*, pp. 73–83. It does not conflict with Kant's or Peirce's characterization of deduction as explicative and not ampliative; rather, it analyzes what explicative means.

3. Roughly, mathematical induction goes like this: k is a member of a series S; there is an operation, say +, by which one can get the next member of the series, k + 1; hence, one can get any member of the series, k + n. Notice that, even though I cannot get all the members of a set (say, all the integers), I can, through mathematical induction, get any member

of the set you please. I cannot get you *all* the integers because there are infinitely many of them, but I can get you any integer that you might choose to have.

4. In this, of course, Mill was in opposition to Hume for whom there could be no objective guarantee that the future will resemble the past. For Hume all that we are warranted to say is that we expect the future to resemble the past because of a constant conjunction (a *de facto* uniformity) in our experience. By association of ideas we come to think of things this way habitually. But we have no reason to think that the uniformity of nature is rooted in any objective necessity.

5. See Peirce, *Collected Papers*, 6.39–41; see 2.761–67 for Peirce's criticism of Mill's theory of induction. See Lonergan, *Insight*, pp. 288ff. for a treatment of the "problem of induction." Finally, see H. E. Kyburg, Jr., "Recent Work in Inductive Logic," *American Philosophical Quarterly*, 1, No. 4 (December 1964), 249-87 for a survey of opinion in this matter, together with an excellent bibliography.

6. See V. G. Potter, *Charles S. Peirce: On Norms and Ideals* (Amherst: The University of Massachusetts Press, 1967), pp. 154ff. for an extended discussion of Peirce's ideas about induction.

7. See Kyburg, "Recent Work," 249–52.

8. My entire treatment of the kinds of inference follows Peirce in the *Collected Papers*, 2.619–25.

9. Ibid., 6.273; see also 6.612; Potter, *Norms and Ideals*, pp. 162-65.

10. Peirce, *Collected Papers*, 7.189–94; Potter, *Norms and Ideals*, pp. 164–65.

11. This entire treatment of abduction is taken from Peirce, *Collected Papers*, 2.632–35.

Study Questions

1. What was John Stuart Mill's objection to deductive inference as a source of knowledge?

2. Discuss what "new" knowledge might mean with respect to deductive inference. Show how this answers Mill's objection.

3. Explain: the conclusion of a deductive inference is formally in the conjunction of the premisses, but only virtually in each premiss taken separately.

4. How would you meet the objection that deduction is trivial because it depends upon propositions which are analytically true?

5. What is understood by "incomplete" induction, and what sort of problem does it pose for philosophers?

6. How did Mill try to justify induction?

7. What is wrong with Mill's justification of induction?

8. What might be a sounder and more sophisticated approach to the "problem of induction"?

9. Show that induction is nothing more than the technique of sampling used in statistical inference. Why is this technique self-correcting?

10. What is one to think of the demand made by some philosophers that the conclusion of an inductive inference be certain?

11. What is abductive inference? Give an example.

12. What is meant by "explanation"?

13. How does one know that an explanation is needed? What sort of cases require explanation?

14. What requirements must be met for an induction to be sound? What requirements must be met for an abduction to yield a probably fruitful hypothesis?

15. Explain the structure of a categorical syllogism.

16. What principle makes the categorical syllogism work?

17. What are the rules for the validity of a categorical syllogism? Explain each briefly.

18. What two forms of hypothetical syllogism are valid?

19. Which forms of the hypothetical syllogism are invalid? Explain why.

20. What is required for a disjunctive syllogism to be valid?

EPILOGUE

Integrative Wisdom

THIS COURSE IN THE PHILOSOPHY of human knowing has proceeded in a rather analytic way; that is, it has broken human knowing down into its various aspects and has tried to show how each contributes to the whole that is the act of human knowing. But it is clear that the acts of human knowing are multiple—in fact, in principle they are indefinitely many. The question arises: Do these acts have or should they have any connection with one another and/or to any overall purpose in human living?

The dynamic desire to know, from which these individual acts of knowing spring, is at the service of a person seeking authentic fulfillment of an entire ongoing and living dynamism. The drive to understand seeks to unify multiple and diverse data, and since in general the final goal of any dynamism must be unity of some kind, the final goal of our cognitive life must be some kind of integration. This means that we must strive to achieve some unified view of the universe and of our place in it. It cannot be enough simply to collect endlessly more and more unrelated data.

Ideally, this noetic integration would be perfectly accomplished by our knowing everything about everything. Practically, however, this cannot be achieved (at least in this life), and so the noetic integration must take the form of a *unified meaning-model* of the universe insofar as we know it. This means a framework in which the *meaning* of the universe is the sense of its *significance*. Such a framework allows the bits and pieces of our knowledge to fit into a universe, a *cosmos*, a meaningful *whole*. It allows me to view my own life within this whole. The attainment of such an integrative vision is sometimes called *wisdom*. To be wise does not require that we know everything about everything, but that we know the place of things relative to each other and to ourselves. It is to know what life as a whole is about. So the ancients called wisdom *architectonic* knowledge, that is, *governing* knowledge because it orders and integrates all the other particular kinds of knowledge.¹ Wisdom orders the universe into a hierarchy of beings and of values. In terms of this ranking wisdom sets the place and worth of man in the universe. In response to this ordering, wisdom mandates an ordering of my own life according to the hierarchy of being and of values. This ordering helps bring about the fulfillment of my nature as the unified center of my aptitudes and potentialities. It is this personal integration of all my drives and capacities into a meaningful unified system which makes a strong, authentic *personality*. This personality shows forth a basic harmony; it is harmony which is the basis of peace. Thus, integration leads to wisdom, which is constituted by harmony and which produces peace.

According to Aquinas, Wisdom in its higher form is a gift of the Holy Spirit and is connected with mystical experience. In its lower form, it is the first philosophy of Aristotle, that is, knowledge of things according to their ultimate causes.[2] In the first case, wisdom supposes a particular religion and theology, and there is no doubt that religious belief is a gift of the Holy Spirit and a source of Wisdom. In the second case, wisdom would suppose a particular metaphysics. Yet what is required is a wisdom that generates the principles upon which metaphysics rests. Hence, a third type of wisdom is required, one based upon a reflective grasp of human understanding in such a way that the invariant structures of human consciousness are appropriated explicitly into one's understanding of oneself and the world. This at once grounds metaphysics and renders religious conviction reasonable. It is perhaps the beginning of wisdom since it provides us with a criterion of the real. Lonergan's "slogan," this volume's epigraph, sums up the positive content of this third sort of wisdom: "Thoroughly understand what it is to understand, and not only will you understand the broad lines of all there is to be understood but also you will possess a fixed base, an invariant pattern, opening upon all further developments of understanding."[3]

Notes

1. This section of "integrative wisdom" is taken largely from W. Norris Clarke's unpublished notes, "Central Problems in Epistemology," pp. 78ff.
2. Lonergan, *Insight*, pp. 407–408.
3. Ibid., p. xxviii.

APPENDIX I

The Fourth Condition

K. Lehrer, in his article "Knowledge, Truth and Evidence,"[1] suggests several possible versions of the fourth condition to supplement justified true belief against the Gettier paradox.

Let "S" stand for the knower; "h" for the true proposition believed; and "p" for some evidential proposition which is in fact false. According to Lehrer, then, the fourth condition might go as follows:

1. It is not the case that S believes h on the basis of any false proposition p; or

2. If S is completely justified in believing any false proposition p which entails the true proposition h, then, he must have evidence sufficient to justify completely his belief in h in *addition to* the evidence he has for p; or

3. If S is completely justified in believing any false proposition p which entails the true proposition h, then S must be completely justified in believing h *even if S were to suppose that p is false*.

Neither the first nor the second will turn out to be satisfactory. I leave it to the reader to find out precisely why, but I will say only that the first version would unduly narrow our knowing, and the second would make our assertion of h dependent upon a conjunction of premisses which is false (and this result is paradoxical). The third version seems to do the job.

Consider the example of the clock in the light of version three. The argument might be summarized thus:

    The clock shows 9 A.M. (true)
    That very clock shows the correct time. (false)
    Hence, the correct time is 9 A.M. (true).

If we suppose that the second premiss is false, then we must correctly conclude that in this case there is no knowledge, because if the second premiss is false there are no grounds at all for believing the conclusion. Hence, the belief is not justified, even if true.

Consider a different example:

Jones who is in my house owns a Ford (true)
Smith who is in my house owns a Ford (false)
Hence, someone in my house owns a Ford (true).

CASE 1: Suppose that I have evidence sufficient to justify my belief in the false premiss, but none to justify my belief in the true premiss. Then according to the third version of the fourth condition I correctly conclude that there is no knowledge in this case, since if I suppose the false premiss to be false (despite the evidence I have in its favor), I have no evidence whatsoever in support of the true conclusion (and hence it is not justified).

CASE 2: Suppose I have evidence sufficient to justify my belief in *both* premisses (the one true and the other false); then the third version of the fourth condition would make me conclude, correctly, that I do have knowledge of the conclusion, even if the second premiss is false, since the first premiss (true and for which I have evidence) entails the conclusion by itself.

Hence, it seems that the proper analysis of "S knows h" is:

1. h is true;
2. S believes h;
3. S is completely justified in believing h;
4. If S is completely justified in believing any false proposition p which entails the true proposition h, then S must be completely justified in believing h even if S were to suppose that p is false.[2]

Roderick Chisholm in Chapter 10 of the third edition of *Theory of Knowledge*[3] offers a solution to the Gettier paradox which relies on the insight that a *false* proposition may be made evident by some other proposition(s) since the relation "to make evident" is non-demonstrative; that is, the propositions which make the false proposition evident to some subject, S, *do not entail* that proposition. Chisholm suggests that such a proposition be called "defectively evident." In our example, then, h would be defectively evident for S if and only if (1) there is an e such that e makes h evident for S, and (2) everything that makes h evident for S makes something that is false evident for S.

Notes

1. *Analysis*, 25 (1965), 168-76.
2. I am indebted to my former student Brian Byrne for pointing all this out to me many years ago in a graduate seminar paper.
3. (Englewood Cliffs, N.J.: Prentice-Hall, 1989).

APPENDIX II

Heelan's Q-Lattice

Heelan takes the exact position language (L_A) and the exact momentum language (L_B) of quantum physics to be the paradigm case of complementarity. Whence he derives the name "Q-Lattice" for "Quantum-Lattice."

Let these two languages be subsets of more inclusive quantum mechanical kinematic language L_{AB} in which the space-time decrisption of a quantum sytsem can be *formulated* (even if, physically, it is impossible to obtain precise *meaurement* of position and of momentum simultaneously).

Two such languages (L_A and L_B) are *complementary* (in L_{AB}) if and only if they constitute part of a non-distributive lattice of language. To contruct such a lattice and to discover its properties, let us first suppose that there is a language L'_A (the logical complement of L_A) which is a development of L_B and a language L'_B (the logical complement of L_B) which is a development of L_A. Next, let us define L_O as the language which entail both L_A and L_B and so is the product of those two (L_{AB}). The lattice would look like this:[1]

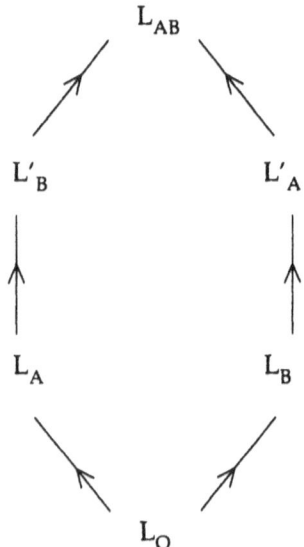

L_{AB} is called the least upper bound (l.u.b.) of the lattice since it is the "least" language implied by both L_A and L_B.
L_O is called the greatet lower bound (g.l.b.) of the lattice since it is "greatest" which implies both L_A and L_B.

One of the unusual features of this lattice is that it is non-ditributive. If it were distributive, then
$L_A + (L_B \times L'_B) = (L_A + L'_B) \times (L_A + L_B)$.
But in our lattice the following relations hold:

1. $L_A + (L_B \times L'_B) = L_A$;
2. $(L_A + L'_B) \times (L_A + L_B) = L'_B$;
3. but it is false that $L'_B = L_A$.

The first relation is true because the product of any set and its complement is always null or empty. The second can be seen to be true by inspecting Heelan's Venn-type diagram produced below. The third relation can be seen to be true in the same way. Yet *if* the lattice were distributive, L'_B and L_A would have to be equal. Consequently, the distributive relation does not hold for the lattice. Hence, it differs from a Boolean lattice where sum *and* product are distributive.

Heelan's Venn-Type Diagram of Q-Lattice

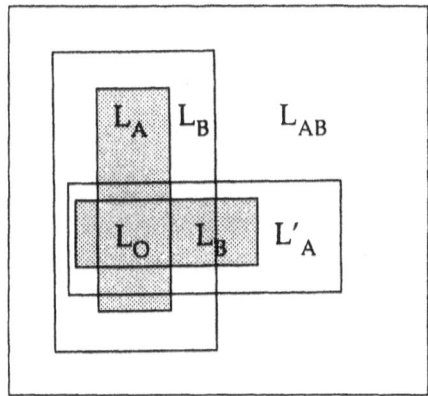

Here is Heelan's own explanation:

> ... Nondistributivity in this case implies that L_A is not identical with L'_B (or L_B with L'_A). In the Venn type diagram, ... the ideal horizon of each tradition is represented by a rectangle, and the partial order, "——>," [see, first diagram in this Appendix] is interpreted as a relation of inclusion: thus L_O is included in L_A, L_B, L'_A, L'_B and L_{AB}; L_A is included in L'_B and L_{AB} but not in L_B and L'_A, and so on. The nondistributive condition then entails that L_{AB} *must* be more comprehensive than L_A and L_B taken separately as pure tradition. Thus, nondistributivity of the lattice signifies that the horizon of the synthesis of two traditions A and B is more extensive than the horizons of the pure traditions A and B, taken separately.[2]

Heelan offers this example of how this lattice might help us understand the relation of complementary philosophical traditions synthesized in a higher viewpoint. He suggest that we excerpt from Aquinas' writings all those passages which are Aristotelian (L_A); let us do the same for those passages in Aquinas which are Platonic-Augustinian (L_B). Yet there would remain another set of Aquinas' texts which are neither L_A nor L_B. Hence, Aquinas' writings are not just the union of Aristotelian and Platonic texts. Aquinas contains them and more.

Notes

1. This and the following figure are taken from p. 183 of Patrick A. Heelan's *Space-Perception and the Philosophy of Science*, copyright c 1983 The Regents of the University of California. I gratefully acknowledge permission to reproduce them here.

2. Ibid., pp. 237–38.

APPENDIX III

Being Mistaken and Being in Error

In a short paper entitled *On Certainty* written at the end of his life, Wittgenstein pointed out the difference between being mistaken and being in error. Frequently enough we use those expressions as interchangeable, and most of the time without any serious confusion since their meanings are related. Nonetheless, according to Wittgenstein, the phrases are synonymous and in some contexts failure to distinguish them can be misleading.

"Being in error," as we have seen, means asserting as true a proposition which in fact is false. "Being mistaken," however, means to have failed in some procedure. One important point of Wittgenstein's reflection on this matter is this emphasis that it is one thing to know and another thing to know that you know. The amount of confidence one has in one's assertions does not, of itself, guarantee that what one believes one also knows. One's mental state (e.g., absolute confidence that one cannot be mistaken) does not constitute one's claim as true. Thus, knowledge is not a mental state that can be detected by introspection (discovering firm conviction) even if knowledge is a state of a subject with a mind.

APPENDIX IV

Derrida and Deconstructionism: A Summary for the Simple

by W. Norris Clarke, S.J.[1]

It is not easy to get at what is really going on in Deconstructionism, because its practitioners are often rather coy in coming out and saying simply and clearly and seriously, "solemnly," what they are doing. Since they are, in fact, cutting all firm, unambiguous links between sign and referent, between thought-language and reality, revealing that no thought or language can just transparently reach out to or lay hold of the real, but always keeps referring obliquely back to itself in reflections of reflections, traces of self, the only thing left to do in the long run is a kind of "play," carefree, somewhat sardonic play with texts, not taking anyone, or at least any text, including themselves, too seriously.

But here is one illuminating way of getting into what they are doing. Look on it as the final *revenge of literature against philosophy*, avenging the ancient slur of Plato, who tried to banish poetry as weaver of unreal images, whereas philosophy gets beyond deceptive images to the real itself, the "really real." Deconstructionism, of whom the grand master is Jacques Derrida in France, has as its aim finally to tear away, unmask, the age-old pretense of philosophy against literature, that is, to reach the objective truth, the real, with clear, literally true, objective concepts, as opposed to the ambiguous image-making of the poet or literary artist. The deconstructionists try to show how all the so-called objective concepts of the philosopher's language (and, hence, thought, which would be mute without language) are really veiled metaphors, images, figural expressions, whose metaphoric character has been repressed, consciously or unconsciously—usually the latter—and masked, passed off, as objective, literal, "transparent" representations of the real itself. There is no firm link in any language between sign and referent, language and reality. Hence, the pretentious claim of the philosopher is really, in the last analysis, when unmasked, just what Nietzsche said was the secret behind all attempts of thought to grasp the real: an exercise of the intellectual *will to power*. Its aim is not truth at all but the secret will to power to impose *my* images on you, my readers. Thus Deconstructionism is the final working out—often openly admitted—of the Nietzschean brand of skepticism ending with the will to power as the only "truth." Since this applies to their own texts too, what is left is to admit this lucidly and then to "play," that is, not take the whole thing, any *text*, too seriously. "Rhetoric" wins out over "logic."

How does one do this unmasking of the truth-pretensions of any human thought (including literature, but especially philosophy, the great pretender to truth)? By *deconstructing* the texts of the philosophers; that is, by a close reading of the text, one spots the surfacing of an image or metaphor whose implications were suppressed and not followed out. Press the metaphor hard, following it out rigorously, and the text cracks upon the long hidden "wound" or fissure; a hidden "shadow text" is exposed, which turns out to be working at cross-purposes to the main surface text—not exactly contradicting it but destabilizing it and rendering it *undecidably ambiguous*, dissolving it into a play of hidden images saying something quite different, against the express intentions of the author. Thus, under every apparently clear, literal surface text lies a not entirely submerged "shadow text" which the deconstructionist brings to light, thus undermining the "authority" of the surface text. This unveiling of the shadow text unmasks the truth-claim pretense of the author as really a veiled intellectual form of the will to power, that is, the will of the author to impose his image or metaphor of the "world" on others.

Any text pretending to objective truth-claims can be thus deconstructed by unmasking its hidden images and metaphors. This does not mean that the deconstructionist has some firm position of his own which he wishes to substitute for the philosopher's. He is rather an infiltrator, a "double agent," a "parricide," who goes in the door of the author and undermines the text *from within*, by pressing hard on the hidden fissure already within the text. Apart from this, the deconstructionist has no truth position of his own; he is fundamentally a "nomad," a wanderer from position to position, text to text, blowing them up blithely as he goes. Thus Prof. Miller, member of the Yale English Department, a center of Deconstructionism, is quoted as describing, with a certain relish it seems, the deconstructionist as a "parricide, a bad son, who has demolished beyond hope of repair the entire machine of western metaphysics." Geoffrey Hartmann of the same school says that despite the surrender of truth involved, this opens up "exciting, vertiginous, possibilities" for new ways of exploring texts.

Note that the deconstructionist is equally at home deconstructing a rationalist like Descartes, a convinced empiricist like Hume, an overly serious logical positivist, an Hegelian, or even the so-called rigorous linguistic analyst (with his method) not excepting the great Wittgenstein himself. Like Nietzsche, Derrida is particularly hostile to the pretensions of Hegel to reach the Absolute Idea, etc. The whole of Hegel's dialectic turns out to be nothing but a brilliantly orchestrated series of images, metaphors, figural references, disguised as genuine objective concepts, imposed on us by Hegel's veiled *will to power*, to be *Master* of truth.

Thus, every philosophical text that makes truth-claims can be deconstructed in two ways: (1) by unmasking the hidden images and metaphors which try to pass off for objective, literal concepts reaching out to the real; and (2) by revealing the hidden shadow text underlying the apparently firm surface text, a shadow piercing through every now and then which works at cross-purposes to and so undermines the surface text by containing a meaning contrary to the author's expressed intention. This destabilizes the surface text and renders its "true" meaning or intent ambiguous, undecidable. Thus, the text begins to work against itself and to crack open, breaking down into internally warring layers. The living whole breaks down into a splintered mosaic of its parts.

For example, much of Western metaphysics insists on *being*, or *presence*, as primary—the *foundation* of all else. But Derrida tries to show how being is actually not primary at all: it can only appear and be known in contrast to *absence, difference*, which turns out to be primary after all. So it is not being, unity, etc. that are primary, for they dissolve into absence, multiplicity, difference as primary. Philosophy seeks for absolute *origins*, foundations, but it turns out that the only way one can understand that something is an origin, *first*, is by contrast with the later, the *second*, and so the second is really first, the later is prior, etc. Nothing holds firm finally; there are no foundations, no center, no absolute source or one; no top, no bottom. Everything shades off into its shadow opposite in a kaleidoscope of reflecting mirrors.

Note

1. This discussion of the application of Deconsructionism to philosophy is taken from Father Clarke's class notes, reproduced here with his permission.

Bibliography

Aaron, R. I. *The Theory of Universals*. Oxford: Clarendon, 1952.

Aquinas, St. Thomas. *Quaestiones Disputatae*. III. *De veritate*. Turin and Rome: Marietti, 1931.

Aristotle. *The Complete Works of Aristotle*. Ed. J. Barnes. 2 vols. Bollingen Series 71. Princeton: Princeton University Press, 1984.

Baier, Kurt. *The Moral Point of View: A Rational Basis for Ethics*. Ithaca: Cornell University Press, 1958.

Black, C. "Knowledge Without Belief." *Analysis*, 31 (1970–1971), 153–58.

Bradley, R., and Swartz, N. *Possible Worlds: An Introduction to Logic and Its Philosophy*. Indianapolis and Cambridge: Hackett, 1963.

Butchvarov, P. *Resemblance and Identity: An Examination of the Problem of Universals*. Bloomington: Indiana University Press, 1966.

Chisholm, Roderick. *Theory of Knowledge*. 3rd ed. Englewood Cliffs, N.J.: Prentice-Hall, 1989.

Clarke, W. Norris, S.J. "Central Problems in Epistemology." Unpublished class notes.

———. "Interpersonal Dialogue: Key to Realism." In *Person and Community: A Philosophical Exploration*. Ed. Robert J. Roth, S.J.. New York: Fordham University Press, 1975. Pp. 141–53.

———. "On Facing Up to the Truth About Human Truth." *Proceedings of the American Catholic Philosophical Association*, 43 (1969), 1–12.

Coffey, P. *Epistemology* I. New York: Longmans, Green, 1917.

Copleston, F. *Friedrich Nietzsche: Philosophy of Culture*. London: Burns, Oates & Washbourne, 1942.

———. *A History of Philosophy* II, III, VII. Westminster, Md.: Newman, 1950, 1953, 1963.

Danto, A. C. *Analytical Philosophy of Knowledge*. Cambridge: Cambridge University Press, 1968.

Delaney, C., Loux, M., Gutting, G., and Solomon, W. D. *The Synoptic Vision: Essays on the Philosophy of Wilfrid Sellars*. Notre Dame: University of Notre Dame Press, 1977.

Derrida, Jacques. *Writing and Difference.* Trans. Alan Bass. Chicago: The University of Chicago Press, 1978.

Descartes, René. *Discourse on Method* and *Meditations.* In *Philosophical Works of Descartes.* Edd. E. S. Haldane and G. R. T. Ross. 2 vols. New York: Dover, 1955.

De Wulf, M. *History of Mediaeval Philosophy.* Trans. E. C. Messenger. 2 vols. London: Longmans, Green, 1926.

Eddington, A. *The Nature of the Physical World.* Cambridge: Cambridge University Press, 1928.

Evans, Joseph Claude. *The Metaphysics of Transcendental Subjectivity: Descartes, Kant and W. Sellars.* Amsterdam: Gruner, 1984.

Gallagher, K. T. *The Philosophy of Knowledge.* New York: Fordham University Press, 1982.

Gettier, E. "Is Justified True Belief Knowledge?" *Analysis,* 23 (1963), 121–23.

Gifford, C. N. *When in Rome: An Introduction to Relativism and Knowledge.* Albany: State University of New York Press, 1983.

Gill, J. H. "Knowledge Is Justified Belief: Period." *International Philosophical Quarterly,* 35, No. 4 (December 1985), 381–91.

Granston, Maurice. *John Locke: A Biography.* Oxford: Oxford University Press, 1985.

Grayling, A. C. *Berkeley: The Central Arguments.* La Salle, Ill.: Open Court, 1986.

Groarke, Leo. *Greek Scepticism: Anti-Realist Trends in Ancient Thought.* Montreal and Kingston: McGill-Queen's, 1990.

Groves, P., and Schlesinger, K. *Introduction to Biological Psychology.* Dubuque: Brown, 1979.

Harrison, J. "Does Knowing Imply Believing?" *Philosophical Quarterly,* 15 (1963), 322-32.

Heelan, Patrick A.. "Hermeneutics of Experimental Science in the Context of the Life-World." *Philosophia Mathematica,* 9 (1972), 101–44.

———. *Space-Perception and the Philosophy of Science.* Berkeley: University of California Press, 1983.

Hintikka, Jaakko. "*Cogito, Ergo Sum*: Inference or Performance?" In *Descartes: A Collection of Critical Essays.* Ed. W. Doney. Garden City, N.Y.: Doubleday Anchor, 1967. Pp. 108–39.

Hume, David. *A Treatise of Human Nature.* Garden City, N.Y.:

Doubleday Dolphin, 1961.
James, William. *Pragmatism*. Cambridge: Harvard University Press, 1975.
John, H. J. *The Thomist Spectrum*. New York: Fordham University Press, 1966.
Kant, Immanuel. *Critique of Pure Reason*. Trans. Norman Kemp Smith. New York: St. Martin's, 1961.
——. *Prolegomena to Any Future Metaphysics*. Trans. P. G. Lucas. New York: Barnes & Noble, 1953.
Katz, Jerrold J. *Cogitations: A Study of the Cogito in Relation to the Philosophy of Logic and Language and a Study of Them in Relation to the Cogito*. Oxford: Oxford University Press, 1986.
Kemp Smith, N. *A Commentary to Kant's 'Critique of Pure Reason.'* 2nd ed. London: Macmillan, 1930.
Kirk, R. *Translation Determined*. Oxford: Clarendon, 1986.
Knowledge and Belief. Ed. A. P. Griffiths. Oxford: Oxford University Press, 1967.
Kyburg, H. E., Jr. "Recent Work in Inductive Logic." *American Philosophical Quarterly*, 1, No. 4 (December 1964), 249–87.
Leach, E. "Structuralism." *The Encyclopedia of Religion*, 14 (1987), 54–64.
Lehrer, K. "Belief and Knowledge." *Philosophical Review*, 77 (1968), 491–99.
——. "Knowledge, Truth and Evidence." *Analysis*, 25 (1965), 168–76.
Leibniz, G. W. *New Essays Concerning Human Understanding*. Trans. A. G. Langley. 3rd ed. 2 vols. La Salle, Ill.: Open Court, 1949.
Locke, John. "An Essay Concerning Human Understanding." In *The Philosophical Works of John Locke*. Ed. J. A. St. John. London: Virtue, 1843.
Lonergan, Bernard J. F., S.J. *Insight: A Study of Human Understanding*. New York: Philosophical Library, 1956.
——. *Verbum: Word and Idea in Aquinas*. Ed. D. Burrell. Notre Dame: University of Notre Dame Press, 1967.
Lyotard, J-F. *The Postmodern Condition: A Report on Knowledge*. Trans. G. Bennington and B. Massumi. Minneapolis: University of Minnesota Press, 1979.
McCarthy, Michael M. *The Crisis of Philosophy*. Albany: State

University of New York Press, 1990.
Maréchal, J., *Le Point de départ de la métaphysique* V. 2nd ed. Brussels: Universelle, 1949.
Maritain, Jacques. *The Degrees of Knowledge*. Trans. G. B. Phelan. New York: Scribner's, 1959.
Mill, John Stuart. *System of Logic*. London, 1843.
Norling, B. *Towards a Better Understanding of History*. Notre Dame: University of Notre Dame Press, 1960.
O'Neill, R. F., S.J. *Theories of Knowledge*. Englewood Cliffs, N.J.: Prentice-Hall, 1960.
Paton, H. J. *Kant's Metaphyic of Experience* I. London: Allen & Unwin, 1936.
Peirce, C. S. *Collected Papers of Charles Sanders Peirce* I–VI. Edd. Charles Hartshorne and Paul Weiss. Cambridge: The Belknap Press of Harvard University Press, 1931-1935.
Philosophical Grounds of Rationality: Intentions, Categories, Ends. Edd. R. E. Grandy and R. Warner. Oxford: Clarendon, 1986.
Philosophy: End or Transformation? Edd. K. Barnes and T. McCarthy. Cambridge: The MIT Press, 1987.
Plato. *The Collected Dialogues*. Edd. Edith Hamilton and Huntington Cairns. Bollingen Series 71. New York: Pantheon, 1963.
Pollock, John L. *Contemporary Theories of Knowledge*. Totowa, N.J.: Rowman & Littlefield, 1986.
Popkin, R. H. *The History of Skepticism from Erasmus to Descartes*. Assen, The Netherlands: Van Gorcum, 1960.
The Possibility of Knowledge: Nozick and His Critics. Ed. S. Luper-Foy. Totowa, N.J.: Rowman & Littlefield, 1987.
Potter, V. G. *Charles S. Peirce: On Norms and Ideals*. Amherst: The University of Massachusetts Press, 1967.
———. *Readings in Epistemology*. New York: Fordham University Press, 1993.
Quine, W. V. *From a Logical Point of View*. 2nd rev. ed. New York: Harper Torchbooks, 1963.
———. "Paradox." *Mathematics in the Modern World: Readings from the* SCIENTIFIC AMERICAN. San Francisco and London: Freeman, 1968. Pp. 200–208.
Rorty, Richard. *Consequences of Pragmatism*. Minneapolis: University of Minnesota Press, 1982.

———. *Philosophy and the Mirror of Nature*. Princeton: Princeton University Press, 1979.
Rousselot, P. *The Intellectualism of St. Thomas*. Trans. J. O'Mahoney. London: Sheed & Ward, 1935.
Royce, J. E. *Man and His Nature*. New York: McGraw-Hill, 1961.
Russell, Bertrand. *The Analysis of Mind*. London: Allen & Unwin; New York, Macmillan, 1921.
Russman, T. A. *A Prospectus for the Triumph of Realism*. Macon, Ga.: Mercer University Press, 1987.
Sartwell, Crispin. "Why Knowledge Is Merely True Belief." *Journal of Philosophy*, 89 (1992), 167–80.
Schacht, Richard. "Nietzsche." *The Encyclopedia of Religion*, 10 (1987), 438–41.
Sellars, Wilfrid. *Science and Metaphysics: Variations on Kantian Themes*. London: Routledge & Kegan Paul, 1967.
———. *Science, Perception and Reality*. London: Routledge & Kegan Paul, 1963.
Shope, R. K. *The Analysis of Knowing: A Decade of Research*. Princeton: Princeton University Press, 1983.
Staniland, H. *Universals*. Garden City, N.Y.: Doubleday Anchor, 1972.
Tarski, Alfred. "The Semantic Conception of Truth." In *Readings in Philosophical Analysis*. Edd. Herbert Feigl and Wilfred Sellars. New York: Appleton-Century-Crofts, 1949. Pp. 52–84.
Truth. Ed. G. Pitcher. Englewood Cliffs, N.J.: Prentice-Hall, 1964.
Unger, P. "An Analysis of Factual Knowledge." *Journal of Philosophy*, 65 (1968), 157–60.
———. "A Causal Theory of Knowing." *Journal of Philosophy*, 64 (1967), 257–72.
Urmson, J. O. *Philosophical Analysis: Its Development Between the Two World Wars*. Oxford: Clarendon, 1956.
Van Steenberghen, F. *Epistemology*. New York: Wagner, 1949.
Warnock, M. *Ethics Since 1900*. 2nd ed. Oxford: Oxford University Press, 1966.
White, Alan R., *Truth*. Garden City, N.Y.: Doubleday Anchor, 1970.
Wittgenstein, L. *On Certainty*. Edd. G. E. M. Anscombe and G. H. von Wright. New York: Harper & Row, 1972.
Wolterstorff, N. *On Universals: An Essay in Ontology*. Chicago: The University of Chicago Press, 1970.

Woozley, A. D. *Theory of Knowledge*. London: Hutchinson University Library, 1962.
Wuellner, B., S.J. "Medium of Knowledge." *Dictionary of Scholastic Philosophy*. Milwaukee: Bruce, 1956. Pp. 74–75.

Index of Subjects

Abduction, 54, 146-47
Abstraction, 6, 44-45, 60, 81-84, 87, 103-105, 110, 114n6, 117-18, 145
Action, 18, 21-23, 61, 109
Analytic, 40, 97-99, 113, 143, 156
Appearance, 15, 52, 61-62, 65, 69-70
A priori, 97-99, 103, 105-13
Association, of ideas, 49, 97, 154n4
Awareness, 22, 31-38, 44-45, 46, 51, 54, 113, 117-18, 134-35
see also Consciousness

Belief, 1, 3-5, 12, 38, 70, 92, 136, 146

Certitude, 3, 8-11, 21-22, 134, 136-37, 138
Cogito, 10, 17-19, 95
Coherence, 120, 122-26
Common sense, 1, 15, 20, 36-37, 39, 45, 47, 55, 61, 95, 99, 123
Concepts, 5, 44, 51, 54, 61, 73, 76-87, 90, 93, 103, 108-10, 113, 116, 119, 135
Conceptualism, 81, 120
Condition, 3-6, 10-11, 18, 31, 47, 50-52, 55-57, 62, 64, 71, 73, 93-95, 105, 107, 141
Conformity, 6, 107, 128n6
Consciousness, 19-20, 35-38, 40, 43, 51, 54-57, 61-64, 68-69, 71, 76-77, 88n6, 90, 95, 106, 113, 131, 134-35
Conversion, in logic, 150-51
Correspondence, 6, 79, 120-22, 125-26, 141-43

Deconstructionism, 28-31, 166-69
Deduction, 53, 147, 151-53
Description, 50-52, 55, 62, 64, 73
Desire, to know, 101-102, 156
Dialogue, 21-22
Doubt, 8-9, 12, 16-19, 23-24, 37, 39

Empiricism, 116-18
Error, 1, 6-7, 9-10, 15, 126-27, 144, 165
Evidence, 2-3, 8-11, 15-18, 20-23, 36-42, 90-94, 99, 111, 125-26, 133, 136-39, 145-46
Experience, 15-16, 21-26, 36-37, 40-42, 44-47, 50-53, 55-57, 61-73, 76, 82, 87, 91-92, 94, 97-99, 103, 105, 107, 113, 130-31, 134-39, 145-47
Explanation, 51-52, 55-57, 62-64, 87, 112-113, 137, 146-47

Falsity (false), 2-3, 5-9, 17-18, 118, 120, 123-26
Form, 6, 41, 103-104, 109, 112, 141, 145-47, 152-53
Framework (viewpoint), 28, 92, 99, 102, 116-119

Idea, 19-20, 36-37, 40-42, 54, 59-60, 62-63, 65-67, 74n6, 79, 97-98, 124-26, 131-32, 137, 154n4
see also Concepts
Idealism, 59-61, 107
Ignorance, 11
Imagination, 46, 131-132
Image, 15, 41, 48, 53, 55, 83, 85-86, 88n6, 90, 103, 131-33;
see also Sensibles

Induction, 53-54, 143-146
Inference, 42, 52, 141, 152-53
Integration, 156-57
Intellect (and cognates), 2-3, 26-27, 41, 82-84, 126-27
Intelligence, 16-17, 38-39, 50-51, 91-92, 102, 111-12, 124-25
Intelligibility, 39-40, 83, 91-94, 106

Judgment, 2-3, 7, 10, 17-18, 23, 38-39, 42, 45, 76, 85, 90-99, 108-13, 125-27, 136

Knowing, 1-5, 7-8, 15-31, 35-42, 44, 51-53, 55-57, 59-60, 62-64, 67-70, 73-74n6, 76-77, 84-85, 90-91, 102-103, 105-13, 123, 130-36
Knowledge, 1-5, 12, 16, 19-21, 24, 27-28, 36, 39-42, 52-53, 60, 63, 68, 85-87, 92, 95-96, 98, 101-102; (memory) 130-36; (testimony) 136-39; (inference) 141-47

Laws, 56, 76, 96, 104-105, 124

Mediation, 52-57
Medium, 55-57, 81-82, 144-45
Memory, 46, 56, 130-36

Nominalism, 61, 79, 80-81, 83-84
Non-Self (non-ego), 19-23, 37, 59-60, 64-65
Noumenon, 106-107, 112-13

Objectivity, 15, 26-27, 38, 61, 64-67, 73, 79, 112, 138
Obversion, 151
Opinion, 3, 10-12, 38, 136

Paradox, Gettier's, 3-5, 159-60
Perception, 44-46, 48-49, 54, 56-57, 62, 67-70, 73, 76, 88n6, 90, 93, 95, 132-33, 135-36
Phenomenalism, 55, 69-73
Phenomenon, 49, 106-107, 112
Postmodernism, 28-31
Pragmatism, 120, 124-26
Predicables, 78-79
Presentation, 38-40, 42, 51, 55-57, 61, 63-65, 67, 91-92, 103, 112
Proposition, 2-3, 5-11, 16-18, 27-28, 85, 90-92, 97-99, 111-12, 120-21, 125-26, 134, 142-43, 148-53

Q-Lattice, 119, 162-64
Qualities (sense), 45-46, 56-57, 60, 63-69, 76, 87

Realism, 59-61, 107, 120
  Direct, 54-57, 61-67, 70-71, 133-36
    Naive, 61-62
    Formal, 62-64
    Virtual, 64-67
  Indirect, 54, 67-73, 132
  Exaggerated, 79-80
  Moderate, 81-87, 103
Reality, 15-16, 21-22, 26-27, 37-38, 60-62, 69, 79, 123, 128n6
Relativism, 26-28, 116-17
Representationalism, 55, 68-69

Self (ego), 19-23, 134
Sensation, 44-57, 59-73, 76, 90, 106-107
Senses, 20, 36, 40-41, 44-57, 61-62, 76, 87, 105-108
Sensibles, 47, 65-69
  see also Quantities

Skepticism, 15-31; 60, 85, 124, 134
Square of opposition, 148-50
Species, 78, 83, 88nn5-6
Structure, of knowing, 35-42; 54, 86, 94, 96-97, 106-107, 112-13, 120, 122, 124; of the eye, 47-50
Subjectivism, 19-23, 60-61, 121
Synthetic, 97-99, 112-13

Testimony, 130, 136-39
True, 1-9, 15, 18-19, 21, 31, 38-39, 94-95, 97-98, 102-103, 126-27, 130-36, (memory) 146-48, 156-57, 159-60
Truth, 1-9, 16-20, 23, 26-28, 31, 40, 52, 90-93, 95, 98, 103, 107, 118-26, 134-38, 145-46, 159-60

Unconditioned, 10-11, 23, 39, 90-91, 93-94, 96, 102, 111, 113, 134
Understanding, 38-39, 41-42, 44, 46-47, 50, 55, 72, 90-92, 98-99, 103-105, 107-110, 112-13, 157
Universals, 61, 76-87, 103

Wisdom, 156-57

Index of Names

Abelard, Pierre, 80, 81
Aquinas, Thomas, 79, 81, 83-85, 101, 106-107, 157, 164
Aristotle, 5-6, 41, 81-83, 101, 106, 109-111, 122, 145, 157
Avicenna, 79, 84
Berkeley, George, 40, 60
Carneades, 16, 30
Chisholm, R., 160
Derrida, Jacques, 30, 166, 168
Descartes, 10, 17-20, 22, 40
Dewey, John, 124-25
Eddington, Arthur Stanley, 15
Einstein, Albert, 28
Fichte, Johann Gottlieb, 29
Galileo, 92
Gettier, Edmund, 3-5, 159-60
Hartmann, G., 168
Heelan, Patrick, 119, 162-64
Hegel, Georg Wilhelm Friedrich, 29, 123, 168
Hume, David, 40, 97-99
James, William, 124-25
Kant, Immanuel, 64, 87, 97-99, 101, 105-13
Lehrer, K., 159
Leibniz, Gottfried Wilhelm von, 40, 106, 128n6
Lévi-Strauss, Claude, 29
Locke, John, 36-37, 40, 55, 64-66, 68, 112
Lonergan, Bernard, 55, 87, 94, 99, 110-13, 157
Lyotard, J.-F., 30
Maréchal, Joseph, 87
Mill, John Stuart, 141, 143-44, 153n1
Miller, J. H. 168

Moore, G. E., 29
Newton, Isaac, 92
Nietzsche, Friedrich, 29-30, 167-68
Ockham, William of, 83-84
Peirce, Charles Sanders, 54, 60, 124, 147
Plato, 1, 3, 79, 166
Pyrrho, 16
Rahner, Karl, 87
Rorty, Richard, 30
Royce, Josiah, 45-46
Roscelinus, 80
Rousselot, Pierre, 87
Russell, Bertrand, 29, 132
Schelling, Friedrich Wilhelm Joseph von, 29
Scotus, John Duns, 83
Sellars, Wilfred, 15, 55, 117
Sextus Empiricus, 16
Steenberghen, Fernand van, 66
Tarski, Alfred, 5-6, 120, 122
White, A., 122
William of Champeaux, 80
Wittgenstein, Ludwig, 29, 121-22, 128n6, 165

www.ingramcontent.com/pod-product-compliance
Lightning Source LLC
Chambersburg PA
CBHW031248290426
44109CB00012B/481